Warrior • 52

US Naval Aviator

1941–45

Robert Hargis • Illustrated by John White

First published in Great Britain in 2002 by Osprey Publishing, Elms Court, Chapel Way, Botley, Oxford OX2 9LP, United Kingdom. Email: info@ospreypublishing.com

ISBN 1 84176 389 6

Editor: Thomas Lowres
Design: Ken Vail Graphic Design, Cambridge, UK
Index by Alan Rutter
Originated by Grasmere Digital Imaging, Leeds, UK
Printed in China through World Print Ltd.

02 03 04 05 06   10 9 8 7 6 5 4 3 2 1

FOR A CATALOGUE OF ALL BOOKS PUBLISHED BY OSPREY MILITARY AND AVIATION PLEASE CONTACT:

The Marketing Manager, Osprey Direct UK,
PO Box 140, Wellingborough, Northants,
NN8 2FA, United Kingdom.
Email: info@ospreydirect.co.uk

The Marketing Manager, Osprey Direct USA,
c/o MBI Publishing, PO Box 1,
729 Prospect Avenue, Osceola, WI 54020, USA.
Email: info@ospreydirectusa.com

www.ospreypublishing.com

Artist's note

Readers may care to note that the original paintings from which the color plates in this book were prepared are available for private sale. All reproduction copyright whatsoever is retained by the Publishers. All enquiries should be addressed to:

John White
5107-C Monroe Rd
Charlotte, North Carolina 28205
704-537-7717,
USA

The Publishers regret that they can enter into no correspondence upon this matter.

Dedication

This book is dedicated to all members of the United States Navy who served in World War II, with a special dedication to the naval aviator and his wings of gold.

Author's acknowledgments

I would like to thank the following people who helped make this book a reality: Mark Henry for giving my name to Osprey as a possible writer; Nikolai Bogdanovic, my commissioning editor, for giving me the chance to be published; Alex Hargis, Sean Hargis, S.J. Sinton, and James Kutch for helping with the composition of the art prints; and last but not least the veterans who helped me with interviews and information: Paul Hoff, R.C. "Pop" Owens, Travis King, Duke Barry, Joe Linick, and all the members of the USS Block Island Association who helped with their input.

FRONT COVER **VF-16 pilots from the USS** *Lexington* **CV-16 celebrate the return from a successful mission against the Japanese-held Gilbert Islands (December 1943). (National Archives)**

CONTENTS

US NAVAL AVIATOR 1941–45

INTRODUCTION: THE FOUNDATION OF CARRIER WARFARE

At military aviation's very beginning, the US Navy command structure saw naval aviation as something of an experiment. Early aircraft were frail and able to fly only in perfect weather conditions. Navy officials hoped that at best aircraft would provide long-range scouting services to locate an enemy, and observation for battleship gunnery once the enemy had been located. Few officers in the US Navy were able to foresee that in less than 25 years the aircraft would become the most decisive tactical weapon in the world.

Admiral William Moffett, appointed Chief of Naval Aviation in 1921 (in the same year that General William "Billy" Mitchell was appointed to head the Army Air Service), saw in aircraft both strategic and tactical potential. World War I had seen the use of the first aircraft carrier and the beginning of strategic bombing; military leaders like Moffett were planning how best to harness the military potential of the aircraft.

Admiral Moffett was, however, in a precarious position regarding the future of naval aviation following the Great War. On one hand he faced opposition from a strong lobby of traditional admirals known as the "gun club" who favored the development of the battleship as the primary weapon of the Navy. These "battleship" admirals hoped to maintain the supremacy of the surface fleet in the wake of the postwar cutbacks in budget that the Navy then faced. Most of theses conservative naval leaders saw naval aviation as a dangerous rival to their beloved battleships, and hardly deserving of a share of the meager funds allocated to the fleet following the war.

Equally difficult for Moffett was the challenge posed by the "prophets" of air power such as General William "Billy" Mitchell, who was so impressed by the potential of aircraft that he was calling for the formation of an exclusive independent air force. For Moffett, with his dreams of a strong naval aviation branch, Mitchell's idea of an independent air force was totally unacceptable. What was needed for all sides was an opportunity to prove the validity of their positions in some kind of test of doctrines and the potential of aircraft.

June 21, 1921 was a warm, balmy day, and the group of military and civilian observers who were gathered for the demonstration was impatient for the experiment to begin. The potential of aerial bombardment was to be tested on a surrendered German battleship that the Navy had provided as a target. Admirals who favored the big-gunned dreadnoughts hoped that the exercise would be a failure, thus dooming once and for all the aircraft in future wars to the role of scouting for the still-supreme battleship. For others there was an air of expectancy to see if the new "prophet" of air power, General Mitchell, would be able to make good his boasts; he had promised in the newspapers that his experimental bombardment group would sink any battleship afloat.

Not to be outdone in this war of words, pugnacious Secretary of the Navy Josephus Daniels offered to stand bare-headed on the bridge of any ship that Mitchell chose to bomb. Seemingly his confidence was not misplaced because the *Ostfriesland*, the target, had already survived not only the worst that the Royal Navy could throw at it during the battle of Jutland in World War I but also 52 bomb hits inflicted by US Navy and Marine aircraft the day before.

The 1st Provisional Air Brigade led by Mitchell arrived over Hampton Roads and began its bombing run. Flying the awkward Martin bombers at an altitude of 1,100 feet, the brigade managed to sink the *Ostfriesland* with just 11 bombs. Naval planners like Moffet were pleased with the results of the tests to the extent that they had shown in a very public way that military aircraft had great potential in naval warfare. The trick, however, was to keep the Navy's aviation branch independent of any combined "air force." In order to forestall this unfortunate development, Admiral Moffett was able to develop a plan for a new combined fleet of heavy and light ships in which the aircraft carrier would play a central part in all strategic situations. Fortunately for Admiral Moffett and his allies, General Mitchell became an unwitting ally in their cause of naval aviation when his undisciplined criticism of his own superiors resulted in his court-martial and suspension from the service in 1925. Henceforth naval aviation would develop as an important integral part of the US Navy, with less hindrance from both the "gun club" and the proponent of a combined service air force.

"Old Glory" waves over the flight deck of the USS *Santee* CVE 29 (Sangamon class) in this November of 1942 photograph as a General Motors TBM "Avenger" runs up its engine prior to air operations. Of primary interest is the narrow width of the flight deck of the CVE "Jeep" carriers. (National Archives)

KEY EVENTS IN THE HISTORY OF NAVAL AVIATION

1910 – Eugene Ely makes first flight off the deck of the USS *Birmingham*.

1918 – The Royal Navy fits a flight deck to a partially complete ocean liner hull to create HMS *Argus*, the first true aircraft carrier.

1921 – General William "Billy" Mitchell's aerial bombing of obsolete battleships proves the versatility of air power.

1922 – The Washington naval treaty is signed limiting the tonnage of capital ships for the maritime nations. Japan and the United States begin to convert former battleship hulls into aircraft carriers. The United States Navy commissions its first aircraft carrier, the USS *Langley*. The *Langley* pioneers the use of internal aircraft repair facilities and new tail-hook arresting gear. Both of these become standard on future aircraft carriers of all nations.

1928 – Two American carriers converted from battlecruiser hulls, USS *Lexington* and *Saratoga*, join the Fleet. They effectively replace the aging *Langley*.

1935 – The Naval Aviation Cadet Act is passed, allowing for increased training of military pilots during peacetime.

1939 – War begins in Europe. The United States declares itself neutral; talk of expanding the Navy begins.

1940 – Commander-in-Chief United States Fleet or CinCUS Admiral Earnest King recommends that all naval aircraft be equipped with self-sealing fuel tanks and protective armor for the pilots.

1940 – The Naval Expansion Act calls for an increase of 1,325,000 in military tonnage and 10,000 aircraft. Known as "The Two Ocean Navy Act" the legislation will increase the size of the Navy by 70 percent.

1941 – Atlantic and Pacific Fleets are established.

Eugene Elly lands his Curtiss aircraft aboard USS *Pennsylvania* in 1911. This is the first heavier than air shipboard landing and began the Navy's long love affair with the airplane.
(National Archives)

1941 – Advanced carrier training groups are established in San Diego and Norfolk.

1941 – USS *Hornet* is commissioned the first ship of Roosevelt's big Navy plan.

1941 – The Imperial Japanese Fleet attacks the US naval base at Pearl Harbor, sinking or heavily damaging many battleships. Fortunately for the United States, the Fleet's aircraft carriers were not present. America declares war on Japan the next day.

1941 – December 10: Aircraft from the USS *Enterprise* attack the Japanese submarine I-70 north of Hawaii. I-70 is the first Japanese vessel sunk by US naval aircraft in World War II.

1941 – The Secretary of the Navy expands pilot training from 800 per month to 2,500 per month, setting a goal of 20,000 pilots by 1943.

1942 – The number of military aircraft is set to 27,500; the Secretary of the Navy announces the V-5 program (V for volunteer) to be held at several American universities, that all prospective naval aviators begin training in a three-month pre-flight course emphasizing physical conditioning.

1942 – The Bureau of Navigation or BUNAV plans for the expansion of pilot training. A new program of training is to last 11 months for the pilots of single or twin-engine planes or 12 months for those of four-engine planes. This change is instituted primarily to lengthen the training program in order to allow the Navy to give the new volunteers military indoctrination prior to flight instruction.

1942 – February 1: The Navy launches its first naval air strike of World War II against Japanese installations on the Marshall and Gilbert Islands. Aircraft from the USS *Enterprise* and USS *Yorktown* carry out the attack.

1942 – April 18: USS *Hornet* launches the Doolittle bomber raid on Tokyo. Japanese naval commanders are shamed by the American attack on the home islands and begin to map out an operation to deal with the US Navy's advanced base at Midway.

1942 – May 4–8: Battle of the Coral Sea. US naval aircraft turn back the invasion of Australia, but USS *Lexington* is sunk in the battle. June 3–6: Battle of Midway, the turning point of the Pacific War. US naval aircraft sink four Japanese aircraft carriers for the loss of one, USS *Yorktown*.

USS *Langley* (formerly USS *Jupiter*) CV1 was the US Navy's first aircraft carrier. Many of the innovations of carrier warfare, such as the flight deck elevator and the aircraft catapult, were tested aboard the *Langley*. (National Archives)

1942 – August 7–Februrary 9: Battle for Guadalcanal. American forces engage in their first major offensive of the Pacific War. Losses of aircraft and ships at one point leave the American navy with only one operational carrier, USS *Enterprise*. Yet in the aftermath of the battle America has gained the initiative in the war that it will never relinquish.

1942 – The training carrier *Wolverine* (IX64), converted from a Great Lakes excursion ship into a flat-top pilot-training platform, is commissioned. Carrier-landing training can now be conducted in the safe waters of the Great Lakes, free from U-boat attacks.

1942 – Naval aviation's first night fighter squadron, the Marine VMF (N)-531, is established at MCAS Cherry Point, NC.

1942 – December 31: USS *Essex* is placed in operating status at Norfolk, Va., the first of 17 ships of that class to be commissioned.

1943 – Naval Reserve Air Bases (NRAB) engaged in primary flight training all over the country are redesigned Naval Air Stations (NAS), but retain the same mission as before.

1943 – February 11: The first combat mission for the Vought F4U Corsair takes place to Vella Lavella as an escort mission by VMF-124.

1943 – Naval squadron designation system changed to scouting squadrons (VS), fighting squadrons (VF), composite squadrons (VC), patrol squadrons (VP), and bombing squadrons (VB).

1943 – The Navy's first night fighter squadron, VF (N)-75, is established.

1943 – Navy designation for aircraft carriers is changed, Saratoga, Enterprise and Essex-type carriers retain CV designation, 10,000 ton- hull light carriers changed to CVL (aircraft carriers, light) and escort carriers changed to CVE (aircraft carriers, escort). And in anticipation of the new 45,000-ton Midway class under construction, the designation is CVB (aircraft carriers, large).

1943 – November 18–26: Occupation of the Gilbert Islands. November 26: Lt. Cdr. Edward "Butch" O'Hare (Congressional Medal of Honor) is killed in a night action against Japanese bombers.

1943 – Naval Air Training Command established at Pensacola, Florida.

1944 – January 29–February 22: The occupation of the Marshall Islands is accomplished.

1944 – Seeing that the end of the war is in sight the Navy begins a reduction in flight training: 1944, 1945 and 1946 at 20,500, 15,000 and 10,000 pilots respectively.

1944 – June 11–August 10: The occupation of the Marianas by Task Force 58 is completed. Japanese losses include the carrier *Hiyo* and two oilers.

1944 – June 24: The Chief of Naval Operations (CNO) outlines new plans for training that will deselect surplus students and extend pre-flight training.

1944 – October 10: The occupation of Leyte. October 23–26: Battle of Leyte Gulf. October 25: Battle of Surigao Strait, and the Battle off Samar Island. In these naval and air actions the effective forces of the Imperial Japanese Navy are destroyed. The first kamikaze attacks are reported against Fleet units.

1945 – Februrary16–March 16: Iwo Jima is captured by Task Force 58.

1945 – March 18–June 21: Okinawa is captured by Task Force 58. USS *Franklin* is seriously damaged by kamikaze attacks. During the course

Aviation Cadets (AvCads) from NAS Corpus Christi check the class-flying schedule in the hangar prior to afternoon flights in this 1942 picture. In the background, aviation mechanics do routine maintenance on this "Yellow Peril" primary trainer at one of the air station's main hangars. (National Archives)

of the campaign, nine different carriers are damaged by Japanese suicide craft. Over Okinawa naval aircraft fly over 40,000 sorties and destroy in excess of 2,500 enemy aircraft.

1945 – August: Atomic bombs are dropped on Hiroshima and Nagasaki, and the formal surrender of Japan is signed on September 2 aboard the USS *Missouri*.

1945 – November 5: Ensign Jake C. West makes the first jet carrier landing aboard USS *Wake Island*.

THE NAVAL AVIATOR: INDUCTION AND TRAINING

Prewar trends and training (1935–40)

The real beginning of naval aviation training for World War II may be traced back to the Great Depression with the passing of the Naval Aviation Cadet Act of 1935. This legislation was part of the "New Deal" policies of President Roosevelt, designed in part to keep the struggling American civil aviation business on its feet as well as increasing the number of potential naval aviators. The central feature of this legislation was the training of reserve officers for the Navy and Marine Corps by providing one year of flight instruction and three years of active duty to qualified college graduates between the ages of 18 and 28.

Air-minded officers saw the changes made in the recruitment and training of naval aviators by the Naval Aviation Cadet Act as an improvement on the previous methods of training. Under the old system only graduates of the US Naval Academy at Annapolis were able to qualify for training as naval aviators and then only after they had served two years with the Fleet as line officers. This stipulation caused many career-minded officers to think twice about an application to a program that would reduce them to the status of trainee. Although precise numbers for this period are very difficult to obtain, the new system turned out fewer, often far fewer, than 100 aviators a month. In 1935, the only year for which figures are available, the entire combined USN and USMC complement of aviators was less than 1,000 pilots, with only 1,500 aircraft of all types.

The first Aviation Cadets, or "AvCads" as they were called, received approximately 800 hours of combined flight instruction and ground school prior to "getting their wings." One major drawback of the new AvCad program was the stipulation that the new pilots serve two years in the Fleet as cadets prior to obtaining commissions in the Navy as ensigns. This feature had been inserted into the program by the Navy partially to alleviate the difficulties of rank senority between the graduates of the Naval Academy and the new AvCads. Under this new system the aviation cadets would be at an age disadvantage for all future promotions vis-à-vis their regularly commissioned brother officers, who would have two full years' seniority over them. The result of course was that the AvCad program failed to attract as many individuals as the Navy wanted.

By the end of 1938 the numbers of naval aviators had been raised to only 1,800 with something over 2,100 aircraft. Modifications to the AvCad program came in 1938 with the introduction of the Naval Aviation Cadet Act. This vital piece of legislation reduced flight training from 12 to six months, limited the ground school from 33 weeks to 18 weeks, and at last gave the new AvCads direct commissions immediately following graduation from flight training.

Wartime training (1940–45)

Let us follow the progress of a typical, though imaginary, potential pilot, John Wright, on the long road to becoming a naval aviator. As a young boy during the twenties in the era of "barn-storming," a whole generation of young Americans fell in love with the romance of aviation. Raised on the stories of "Captain Eddy"(Captain Edward Rickenbacker) and the exploits of the "Lone Eagle" Charles Lindbergh, these young college students were eager to share in the glory of the exploration of the air.

For a young man like John, his initial flight instruction might have come from the Civilian Aeronautics Authority Civilian Pilot Training Program, or CAA-CPT. This program started in 1939 at 12 colleges around the country and was designed to increase the number of potential pilots in case war broke out. The class cost was minimal, about $25, and provided the trainee 40 hours of flight time in small civilian planes and about 70 hours of ground school. At the end of the course the student took a basic flight test with a CAA inspector and received his private pilot's license. The CPT did not require the new pilots to assume a military obligation, but it did provide the basis for many new aviators' entry into the military as December 1941 approached.

Many young men (65,000 by 1945) like John Wright began their military career at one of the nation's Naval Reserve Air Bases (NRABs).

Intermediate flight training of AvCads continued in the North American SNJ Texan, an advanced flight trainer. These pilots walk across the tarmac at NAS Pensacola in early June 1942, geared up in their parachutes. (National Archives)

Known as "E bases" by the trainees ("E" for elimination, because the failure rate was as high as 30 percent among the new pilots), the trainees received 30 days of flight instruction as seaman recruits. The cadet candidates, who had to have completed a minimum of two years at college and have logged at least 10 hours of flight time, were subjected to a series of physical and basic educational tests in what was essentially a "boot" camp designed to weed out those clearly unfit to be pilots or officers.

At the E base the new seaman recruits were taught the basics of aviation, such as the names of the various parts of an aircraft. Close-order drill was taught, as well as the basics of military discipline.

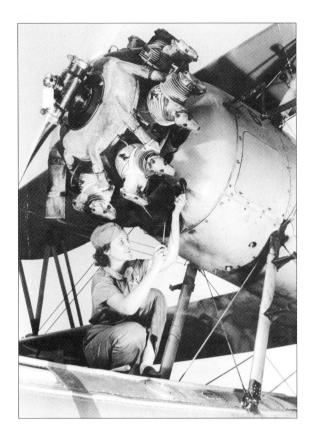

As the need for pilots grew so did the need for aviation mechanics. This USN WAVE (US Navy woman mechanic) works on the radial engine of one of the training command's "Yellow Peril" floatplanes c.1942–43 (National Archives)

The curriculum of the E base included engine repair, radio and Morse Code skills, and some lessons in elementary navigation and instrument flying. The E bases concentrated on training for military life at the expense of aviation; as one future naval aviator put it, the recruits learned more about washing down airplanes and cleaning heads (latrines) than they did about flying.

Having completed his E-base training, Seaman Wright was then sent on the second part of his program to become a naval aviator, Naval Air Basic Training at NAS Pensacola, the "cradle of naval aviation." Here the aviator hopeful was discharged as a seaman and enrolled as a naval air cadet. Cadet Wright was signed to a contract under which he was to receive the sum of $75 a month plus room, board, and uniforms.

Discipline for the young cadets was a delicate situation; technically they were neither officers nor enlisted men, yet by naval tradition they were entitled to be called "Mister" and treated like gentlemen. In the prewar Navy, with its strong traditions of anti-fraternization with enlisted men, the AvCad defied categorization, being neither fish nor fowl as it were. Coupled with the fact that there were also enlisted pilots in the service, known by the rank of Naval Air Pilot (NAP) rather than the more prestigious Naval Aviator, some surface force officers had a difficult time relating to the aviation branch officers who had such close dealings with both mechanics and NAPs.

While at NAS Pensacola a new cadet like John Wright would pass through three separate squadrons where he would advance from basic to advanced levels. In the Navy the philosophy was and is that the naval aviator must be more than a pilot: he must also have a working knowledge of both the theory and the mechanics of aircraft. Classes were given in navigation, communication, engines, and meteorology as part of the ground school curriculum (academic classes of non-flying nature). Eventually the new aviator would be able to master all aspects of flying and the maintenance of aircraft. According to several sources the training at Pensacola was like several years of graduate-level work at a university due to the advanced nature of the classes given to the AvCads in such a short period of time.

For John and the other new AvCads the flight training began with primary instruction in land-based aircraft that was to last three months; this was where the cadet was introduced to the N3N basic trainer. Up to this point in his career Cadet Wright had flown in small, easy-to-fly aircraft like the Piper J-3 Cub, a high-wing, fabric-covered monoplane with a 50 hp engine. The N3N, also known as the "Yellow Peril" with its 300 hp engine, was a different proposition altogether, being a fully acrobatic biplane. The nickname "Yellow Peril" was based in part on the plane's bright shade of yellow paint, but it also referred to the very real possibility that many new cadets were likely to be in peril of "washing out" of the program.

One of the most common forms of teaching the principles of aerial gunnery took place on the skeet range. For the rear seat gunners this practice often continued well into the cruise, with skeet competitions being held off the "fantail" of the ship. (National Archives)

In primary flight instruction the cadets were taught the rudiments of flying, with tests or "checks" being given at 20, 40, and 60 hours flying time by instructors known as "check pilots." These check flights were designed to monitor the progress of the cadets in the vital skills of flying such as recovering the plane from a stall and basic air maneuvers like takeoffs and landings.

One of the major complaints of the cadets was the highly subjective nature of the grading during the check flights. In order to get a passing score the cadet needed to perform the required maneuver so as to satisfy his instructor as to the cadet's competence as a pilot. These check pilots, being former AvCads themselves who upon graduation had been assigned the less than desirable duty of flight instruction, were apt to be difficult to please.

Following his check flight Cadet Wright, who had received an "up" check, was allowed to go on in his instruction. Those of his comrades who were given a "down" check were assigned additional study time before being given a second chance to pass the test prior to washing out of the program. In total the primary squadron gave the fledgling pilots 90 to 100 hours flight time in which to master the basics of flight.

If he was lucky, the next step in the training process for Cadet John Wright was the second squadron known as intermediate flight instruction, where he was taught formation flying and aerobatics. Intermediate flight instruction lasted four months. At this point the cadet began to specialize in aircraft of his own choosing, such as floatplanes, multi-engine aircraft, or, the most prized of all, carrier aircraft. Ground school instructions became more difficult with the introduction of more advanced concepts of navigation and radio communication, and the number of solo hours of flying was increased to 160. Likewise, training flights were now conducted in larger and more powerful aircraft, like the SNV Valiant (known as "the Vibrator") and the famous North American SNJ Texan, both of which were low-wing monoplanes with engines rated at 600 hp.

During this intermediate phase of training Cadet Wright would be evaluated and selected for one of the three types of flying duty to which a new ensign could be assigned: multi-engine (VP), battleship/cruiser (VO) training, or carrier (VC) training. The evaluation of the cadets was based on their perceived strengths as noted by their instructors and by the preferences stated by the trainees themselves. Of all the possible choices, the VC squadrons were the ones that the cadets wanted to join, being the most glamorous and flying the Navy's newest aircraft.

Following a successful up-check from the intermediate squadron, Naval Air Cadet Wright entered the final stage of his training. The third squadron provided advanced or what was known as operational training to the cadets. Instruction in instrument flying was supplemented, with the student being introduced to the notorious "black box," the link trainer. The link trainer was a small replica aircraft in which the trainee was seated; a technician could remotely control the link to simulate a variety of situations that could occur while flying on instruments. The cadet's test was to control the link trainer in the same manner as he would an actual aircraft while on instruments, eventually landing the craft safely.

Much of the operational training for the carrier squadrons was done at NAS Opa-Locka near Miami, Florida, where the instructors were veteran Fleet pilots skilled in the arts of dive-bombing, gunnery, fighter tactics, and aerial navigation. Each of the advanced students was given opportunities to hone his skills in the areas of carrier operations, fighters, dive-bombers, and torpedo bombers before final selections for squadron placement of the cadets were made.

The students were now given the rudiments of basic carrier procedures, touch-and-go landings, as well as simulated carrier deck landings with a painted deck on the actual runway. As Cadet Wright progressed, he was taught the basics of aerial gunnery by the use of a target device know as a "sleeve." The target sleeve was towed at a speed of approximately 150 mph by another fighter aircraft, and the students would practice the art of deflection shooting, firing at a moving target from an angle. The bullets of the various gunners were tipped in different colors of paint in order to record more easily the hits scored by each respective cadet.

The second stage of the operational training allowed the cadets to try their hands at the art of dive-bombing. For this part of their training the cadets would fly the Curtiss SBC-3 "Helldiver," the last of the Navy's biplane attack craft. The "Helldiver" was an aging craft powered by a 750 hp engine that had a maximum speed of only 220 mph.

For the training exercise the target was a 50-foot bull's eye within a 100-foot circle. Successful attacks required three out of five attempts within the ring to earn a passing score.

Torpedo practice was often dispensed with during operational training due to a lack of suitable available aircraft. Only recently had the Navy begun to make the Douglas TBD "Devastator" operational within the Fleet and very few of these craft were available to the training command. This missed opportunity for experience with the

Hollywood played its part in the war effort. Here actor Robert Taylor poses in front of his SNJ Texan wearing the winter flying suit of the US Navy. (National Archives)

torpedo would cost the US Navy dearly in the initial stages of the carrier wars, since the Navy's prewar torpedo was of a faulty design which extensive prewar training usage could well have revealed.

At the end of the operational training program, Cadet John Wright was at long last able to graduate and take on the title of naval aviator, with the rank of ensign. United States Naval tradition required that new officers gave a silver dollar for the first salute received. Many were earned by wily drill instructors as they gave their former charges their first salute on the way back from the graduation parade.

By the time of graduation the new ensign would already have been selected by his instructors for a specific type of assignment and would be given appropriate advanced training. For example, a carrier assignment would be in one of three types of carrier squadron: fighters (VF), dive-bombers (VB), or torpedo bombers (VT). Starting in 1941 the new aviators could also be assigned to a new type of combined squadron, the composite (VC), that flew all three types of carrier planes off the Navy's new smaller carriers, the CVGs, or jeep carriers.

Prior to final assignment to a carrier-based squadron, however, the new aviator would receive further instruction at the advanced carrier-training group (ACTG). Here they would be evaluated by pilots of the Fleet and given the opportunity to "get some salt water on their wings," i.e., qualify on carrier deck landings. Due to the increased need for carrier pilots with the outbreak of war, and in view of the paucity of training time, carrier qualification training was set at eight actual carrier landings.

On December 7, 1941 news of the Japanese attack on Pearl Harbor reached all Fleet units by the shocking radio message "Air raid Pearl Harbor, this is no drill." War was declared the next day on Japan and America's aviators, like the rest of her military forces, would undergo the most difficult test they ever faced.

CARRIER ASSIGNMENT: SHIPBOARD LIFE

In the 1940s living conditions aboard a US naval vessel, even as large a carrier as the new USS *Essex* (820 feet long), were cramped and confined by civilian standards, with over 2,500 men aboard the ship. For the newly minted ensign like John Wright life on a carrier could come as a series of surprises. The fledgling officer's initial awe at the size of his new navy gray home with its maze of companionways and ladders would give way to claustrophobia after a few short weeks. For ensign Wright and other new aviators the only time that he might have been on a ship was during his carrier qualification landings and even then he had not been out of his fighter. Naval aviation training had focused solely on the flying aspects of the service, so life on board a Navy vessel could not fail to be full of new experiences.

Perhaps the greatest of these surprises came in the sleeping arrangements, called berthing by the US Navy, when the pilots found out exactly how confined they would be. Firstly, the aviators did not live together on board the ship because of the possibility of a single hit killing a large number of the air group at one time. Commanders, lieutenant commanders, and the senior lieutenants were assigned semi-private cabins along with the rest of the senior officers of the ship, where they might share cabin space with one or two roommates depending on the numbers and ranks of the senior officers present.

Living conditions aboard a carrier were crowded for all ranks. Here an officer takes a moment to write a letter home from the confines of the junior officers' berth. (National Archives)

These semi-private cabins were small airless gray rooms, approximately ten by ten feet with a locker and bed for each inhabitant and a desk and chair that had to be shared by all of the room's inhabitants. The deck of the cabin was rough navy gray steel, which was very unforgiving to anyone unlucky enough to fall onto it from a bunk during stormy weather, and the ceiling was crisscrossed with a variety of conduits and pipes that were a hazard to the heads of sleepers in the upper bunks.

The ordinary pilots, along with the other officers of the ship's company (ensigns through to lieutenants [junior grade]), were given berths in the junior officers' bunkrooms. Known as the "Black Hole of Calcutta" by its residents, the junior officers were housed in very close quarters, sometimes with as many as 12 men in a room sleeping in bunks set in tiers at the standard Navy regulation 18 in. vertical clearance, a privacy curtain being the only distinction to an officer's bunk. Like most of the rooms on aircraft carriers the "Black Holes" were not air-conditioned, so sleeping conditions could be most uncomfortable due to the close proximity of one's bunkmates.

During the long ship's crossing from the Pacific coast of the United States to the war zone, time often weighed heavily on the young officers. Ensign Wright, sweating in the hot darkness of the Black Hole, spent his time trying to figure out some way to make his and the life of all the other junior officers berthed with him more comfortable. Not far away was one of the ship's air-conditioning lines that supplied cool air for one of the other squadron's ready rooms; the only problem was how to reach the line and vent some of the air into the bunkroom. With the inventiveness that is born of desperation the junior officers built an air duct from the covers of old instruction manuals and taped the section together, while others of their group cut their way into the main air-conditioning duct. As the cool air now filtered into the room Ensign Wright and the rest of the junior officers rested more comfortably knowing that they had earned a " job well done," having used their resourcefulness in desperate times.

Most of Ensign Wright's time was taken up with training and instruction, but not all his days were the same. A very special day occurred if the ship neared the Equator, and veteran members of the crew prepared for an old Navy ceremony known as "Crossing the Line." This was actually a series of events in which those who had crossed the Equator before, "shellbacks," prepared to initiate those who had not, "pollywogs," into the kingdom of Neptunus Rex, ruler of the deep.

In this 1945 picture aboard USS *Hornet* CV 12 a group of VF 11 pilots while away the hours with a card game in the ready room prior to a mission to Japan. All the pilots wear the late-pattern AN life jacket and carry pistols in shoulder holsters. (National Archives)

The crew of the carrier engage in calisthenics. During non-flight hours, games of baseball could be played on separate portions of the flight deck. (National Archives)

While not all ceremonies were identical from ship to ship, all had certain features in common. Each mess or department handled its own pollywogs in pre-initiation ceremonies that usually started two days before the main event, Crossing Day. The shellbacks convened a court, made up of the Grand Inquisitor (a direct representative of Neptune) and Davy Jones acting as scribe. The rest of the court consisted of assistant inquisitors and sundry kibitzers (a term that applied to any shellback that was not an official of the court) who tried the pollywogs and found them guilty on charges dealing with a pollywog invasion of the realm of King Neptune. On the day following the trial the pollywogs were given to the charge of various shellbacks and given whimsical tasks to perform, like "iceberg watch," which the pollywog was obliged to perform wearing his warmest winter clothing.

On Crossing Day, Davy Jones appeared with full pomp and circumstance, accompanied by King Neptune, his Queen, and the royal baby (the fattest man on the ship). At this point the pollywogs were introduced to the royal court, and anointed with various noxious substances. The pollywogs genuflected to the court and then ran the gauntlet of the assembled shellbacks, who give them each a solid whack on the buttocks with a paddle as they ran down the line. At long last the pollywog had become a shellback, and on the next crossing these same rites would be passed on to the next generation of new sailors.

Due to the uncertain nature of service at sea during wartime, meals were served three times a day, with a two-hour period in which a man could get his food. Meals for the officers were conducted by rank in the officers' wardrooms. Senior officers were served at their own green-baize-covered tables by mess stewards while the ensigns served themselves and ate apart from their commanders in a separate facility. For example, on days of heavy flight operations an "early bird" breakfast was held at 0400, at least an hour before the rest of the crew, for the pilots, aircrews, and other members of the air division. By modern standards the breakfasts were somewhat protein heavy, consisting of steak, bacon, ham and eggs, the portions were plentiful and the men could eat as much as they wanted. At any time of the day coffee was available; indeed the coffee was so plentiful that it was known as the ship's emergency boiler. The other meals were served in the same manner as breakfast, yet on this one point the US Navy was absolutely equal: the officers ate the exact same quality of rations as the men.

Several hours of each day were spent by the new pilots in the squadron's ready room, engaged in lessons taught by the senior officers. Here the new ensigns would add the squadron experiences of battle-hardened pilots to what they had been told by their flight instructors. Hard-learned lessons of the Coral Sea and Midway battles were recounted as the training of the new pilots intensified.

While on active duty, sailors from the Fleet had to spend their shore leave time on unimproved island facilities. In this 1944 picture sailors relax with a few beers on Mog Mog Island, a coral atoll near Ulithi. (National Archives)

Built to accommodate 24 to 36 pilots, every squadron aboard the ship had at least one ready room for its pilots. Because of the size of their aircrews torpedo and dive-bomber squadrons were given two ready rooms for flight operations, one for officers and one for enlisted personnel. The ready rooms were some of the most comfortable on the carrier, having air-conditioning as well as leather easy chairs. Hung along the walls of the ready room were parachute harnesses, leather flight jackets, helmets, and other flight gear that the pilots might snatch at a moment's notice. At the front of the long narrow room hung the chalkboard that the squadron commanders used for briefings prior to air operations. Maps of the combat area, full-scale models of island targets, and models of enemy ships and aircraft littered the room. It was here in the ready room that the pilots gathered, compared notes on previous missions, and wrote their action reports. Lessons on attack methods were taught to the younger pilots by their commanders, and between missions the aviators sweated out the long hours of waiting with cards and games of Acey-Duecy.

In the Pacific War the centerpiece of the naval air effort against Japan was the aircraft carrier. Unlike other ships of the line, carriers were never what could be described as "taut ships." Rather the special nature of their daily operations, with the need to react to any and all situations, made life and discipline on a carrier different from those on other types of US Navy vessel. For example, an Essex-class carrier, with a crew complement of over 2,500, was more like a small city afloat than a ship, and captains had to be able to allow the various experts to do their jobs effectively.

Air operations too demanded a special level of interaction between enlisted men and officers. Like a complicated ballet production, pilots, aircraft handlers, ordnance men, and flight operations crewmen needed to work smoothly as a team. Enlisted personnel would be called upon to give directions to officer pilots that had to be followed for the easy functioning of the operation. Plane handlers and other deck crew had to be aware of all kinds of hazards, from the whirling props of the planes to the movement of the ship's elevator, and had to make important decisions about both men and equipment without being told to do so. All in all the group of men involved in the air operations of the carrier had to be men of independent thinking who could be relied upon to make important judgments on their own initiative.

Perhaps one of the most interesting characteristics of the aviators was their willingness to admit to fear during air operations and combat sorties. What might almost be called a "cult of fear" arose, with many flyers telling stories of exactly how afraid they had been during any given set of circumstances.

The Navy has a just reputation for serving the best food of all the military branches, but at general quarters the crew was served meals of sandwiches and coffee while at stations. The central figure is a "blue shirt" or plane handler from the USS *Lexington* CV 16, 1944. (National Archives)

The greatest example of this spirit occurred on a daily basis in the ready rooms of thousands of Naval installations, from Dutch Harbor in the Aleutians to Henderson Field in the Solomons, where naval aviators gathered to discuss their most recent missions. At these debriefings and in their written "after action" reports, aviators were urged to report the events of the mission exactly as they had occurred, without "gun decking" (making exaggerated claims of success). The immediate purpose of debriefings was of course to learn from past mistakes, yet they also served to build morale and teamwork through the catharsis of reliving fear and then coming to terms with it. One naval aviator, when speaking of air combat, put it this way: "Brother, my pants were wet and I didn't hardly have the strength to pull the trigger. But I managed to pull it."[1]

Ship's companies, and squadrons especially, are by necessity tightly knit groups: the survival of all is often dependent on the performance of the individual. To the casual observer this clannishness seems to be unnecessarily exclusive, amounting to unfriendliness, yet it played an important role in the psychological makeup of the group. By their very natures newcomers possess unknown and untried qualities. And if the newcomer is a replacement for a lost comrade, then the situation becomes even more charged. Often veterans would not want to know even the names of the new men, in an effort to avoid the pain of future bereavement. This attitude was not an attempt by the veterans to be cruel to the replacements, but was rather an attempt to cope with the realities of war. One of the flight surgeons on the *Essex* made his feelings clear when he said:

> I made the mistake of knowing those fellows, hanging around the Ready Rooms and making lots of friends. They were great guys. We had some good laughs. Then, when they started turning up missing, or when they flopped in on the deck so badly wounded we could do little or nothing for them, it got me down … that was too hard a dose to take, so I made up my mind I wouldn't make friends among this group.[2]

Service men have always felt that the folks on the Home Front did not know or did not care about what conditions the military might be enduring, and the naval aviator was no exception. In the Pacific the carrier crews thought all the war news focused excessively on Germany, while the Atlantic crews, on their long convoys, would tire of hearing about the "great" carrier battles in the Pacific. One American sailor summed up the attitude of his fellows well by saying:

Two aviators relax with sandwiches and coffee following a "hop" in the Pacific. A notable point in this photograph is the China, Burma, India patch on their flight suits. Rarely during World War II did naval aviators wear devices on their flight suits. (National Archives)

I get letters from home saying the papers don't talk much about our war … everything Germany, Germany, Germany. That's ok, too. It doesn't make any difference to me whether they even know we have a Navy. Publicity don't win any fights for you and I never heard of a Fire Control man second class getting a Navy Cross.[3]

Nevertheless, whether in the Atlantic or the Pacific, north or south of the Equator, stationed on a massive aircraft carrier or at the smallest outpost in the most remote corner of the world, the naval aviator was on hand to do his job, regardless of what the newspapers said.

Meanwhile, as the carrier traveled closer toward the war zone, the pace of training for all hands increased. Full-scale air strikes were planned and practiced by the attack squadrons, gun crews were given ceaseless drill, and aircraft spotting and anti-aircraft target practice were conducted by all hands.

New ensigns have at all times been viewed as the lowest form of life in the Navy. This certainly was true of a green pilot newly assigned to a fighting squadron in time of war; the new ensign was in for a certain amount of scrutiny and "hazing" or good-natured joking about their skills as aviators from his fellow pilots until he proved himself. Indeed the newest ensigns assigned to squadrons were extra pilots without an aircraft of their own. For Ensign Wright and other rookie pilots, flight time was made up in the most routine assignments: practice carrier deck landings and flying as the inner antisubmarine patrol, a tedious mission where the pilot flew long racecourse circles scanning the ocean for the wake of either torpedoes or that of the periscope of a submarine.

Lieutenant Commander John S. Thatch, the commander of fighter squadron three (VF 3), in order to give additional instruction to his pilots kept what he called a "humiliation team," composed of four members of his squadron, to test new pilots in dog-fight situations. Thatch's aim was to prove to the new "hot shots" that they still had a lot to learn about being fighter pilots. Thatch and his team were famous for pulling stunts like eating food in the cockpit and reading newspapers while dog fighting with the new pilots, just to show how easy it would be for the team to shoot down the new pilot if they really wanted to.

The one factor that remained constant for Ensign Wright and all the other naval aviators whether they had four hours' flying time or over 4,000 was the constant training for the fight that was to come.

Two naval aviators pose in front of the Talley board of VF-17 in 1944, also know as the "Jolly Rogers" it was under the command of Tom Blackburn and was the first Navy squadron to fly the F4U Corsair in combat.

BELIEFS AND BELONGING

The young men like Ensign John Wright who became aviators to fight the war were still civilians at heart, and they did not see the Navy as a career; they still planned to return to civilian life after it was all over. For most of these men the war would be the defining moment of their lives, or as one naval aviator put it:

> I've got to make some sort of career [after the war] for myself, knowing all the time that my real career is behind me, knowing that everything I do is dull and unimportant after you've laid your bombs carefully on Rabaul and Wake and Marcus and Truk and Bougainville … I don't see how I can ever get excited about making the next dollar.[4]

The US Navy had always held an attraction for men longing to see the exotic far corners of the world, yet during time of war sailors might be stationed in anything but romantic settings. Ships' chaplains, responsible for maintaining the ships' libraries, found themselves inundated with requests from the crew for magazines and books about the areas that the ship was cruising.

During the numerous air operations performed by the US Navy during World War II pilots were sometimes shot down and in need of assistance. In this photograph a "Hellcat" pilot has his picture taken with the pilot and aircrew of an OS2U "Kingfisher" from USS *Baltimore* CA-68 that rescued him from Truk lagoon in March 1944. (National Archives)

Initially many of the US Navy recruits were young men to whom the Japanese attack on Pearl Harbor was the motivating factor in their decision to enlist. Air crewman R. C. Owens put things this way:

I personally was very mad at the entire [Japanese] nation for what they did at Pearl Harbor. I had no remorse about the "enemy" that we killed in the line of duty, be it shooting down airplanes, strafing or bombing ground personnel, trains, bridges, ships or any other target. It served them right for what they sneakily did to our nation at Pearl Harbor. We were young and had no fear about dying or killing them. Well, when I saw the smoke from cannon fire from the wings of the Jap fighters I did tighten up a bit."

Team work and fighting spirit were an integral part of naval aviation, many of the US Navy's greatest successes stemming from this esprit de corps among the aviators. Here VF-16 pilots from the USS *Lexington* CV-16 celebrate the return from a successful mission against the Japanese-held Gilbert Islands (December 1943). Of particular interest are the non-regulation decorations on the squadron's flying helmets, such as the red helmet stripe on Lt. Cdr. Paul D. Buie's (fourth figure from left) khaki flying helmet, and the black shamrock visible on the helmets of two other pilots. (National Archives)

Yet as the war wore on, many US Navy sailors viewed the war as a job that had to be mastered if they were to survive. Nevertheless, a common thread in the belief system of the naval personnel of World War II was an intense dislike, if not outright hatred, of the Japanese: "The only thing that I know for certain is what we are fighting against. We're fighting to kill these bastards before they haul off and kill us." (an unknown sailor in the Pacific).[5]

US forces were rarely able to come into close contact with Japanese naval personnel because so many Japanese units chose death over surrender. Even when Japanese aviators or aircrew were taken prisoner it was not uncommon for them to attempt to kill themselves while in captivity. Each side in the Pacific War could respect the skill and courage of the other, but neither side was ever truly able to understand what "made the other guy tick." Divided along lines of race, religion, and custom, the Americans and the Japanese found little in common and as a consequence it was far easier for them to hate each other.

However, this hatred between the two combatants did not prevail in the Atlantic. The war there was fought every bit as ferociously as that in the Pacific, but in the Atlantic survivors from destroyed German submarines were taken aboard US naval vessels when possible. Upon

Work aboard a US Navy carrier was a 24-hour-a-day job. Here on the hangar deck ordnance crew (foreground) prepare 1000 lb bombs to be loaded on the SBDs, while officers and men in the background relax in front of a movie.

Here a TBM "Avenger" makes a slow practice run and launches a Mk. XIII torpedo. Later in the war the performance of the Mk. XIII was improved by the addition of nose and tail drag devices that allowed the torpedo to be delivered from higher altitudes, and at faster speeds (1942–43). (National Archives)

closer contact with enemy seamen US sailors in the Atlantic found them not too different from themselves. Navy chaplain Sheridan Bell of the USS *Card* (CVE 11) noted the behavior of US and German seamen at the funeral of the commander of the German submarine U-233, Kaptain-leutnant Hans Steen, who died from his wounds following a prolonged effort on the part of surgeons to save his life:

> The service was an interesting one because of the spirit of both companies. Each time that we have had survivors aboard, there has been a noticed interest on the part of our own men that they share their cigarettes and their candy and their ice cream with the prisoners of war, do not look on them as enemy but as sailors who are then in need and there is no sense of bitterness or hostility.[6]

AIRCRAFT OF THE FLEET, 1941–45

During the war years the US Navy used several aircraft to serve the needs of the Fleet and its aviators. No study of those pilots would be complete without some brief mention of the aircraft they flew.

The Grumman F4F Wildcat

When the war started the US Navy had two new monoplane fighters that were being tested prior to full-scale contracts being issued to reequip the Fleet. The first of these fighters was the Brewster F2A Buffalo, but the one that won the contract was the Grumman F4F Wildcat. An obsolete design by the time the war started, the F4F was destined to carry the burden of fighter combat until 1943. This small stubby fighter, 28 feet long with a wing span of 38 feet, was inferior in most respects to the Mitsubishi Zero fighter. Yet in spite of these difficulties the Wildcat possessed several virtues that allowed the highly trained American aviators to take on the Japanese on something like equal terms.

First the Grumman fighter had a better weapons battery then the Zero: four .50 caliber machine guns (later increased to six) compared to the Zero's two 7.7 mm and two 20 mm cannon (later increased to four). The power of the American .50 caliber was a big factor in several early combat operations against the Japanese. Japanese aircraft without the benefit of sealed fuel tanks had a nasty tendency to burn after only a few bursts of fire. Unlike the Zero the F4F had an armored bulkhead behind the cockpit, which meant that it was able to take tremendous punishment and still bring its pilot home, thus keeping American pilot losses below that of the Japanese.

The Grumman F6F Hellcat

Beginning in 1943 the US Navy was being equipped with a new carrier fighter that would carry on the tradition that was started by the Wildcat. This latest addition from Grumman was the F6F Hellcat. Proportionally larger than the Wildcat, the F6F provided marked improvement in all areas of performance over its predecessor. With the introduction of the Hellcat the Navy was at last able to begin to conduct offensive air operations that were designed to give them air superiority over the Japanese.

Like most American fighters, the robust Hellcat design allowed it to conduct a wide variety of missions that involved carrying many different types of ordnance; at one point the Navy even experimented with turning the Hellcat into a torpedo bomber. Indeed the versatility of the fighter-bomber design proved the death knell of the three-plane air groups, with their combination of torpedo bombers, dive-bombers, and fighters; with one plane type the Navy would be able to conduct the same types of missions in the postwar years.

The Chance Vought F4U Corsair

Perhaps the most innovative US Navy fighter developed during the war, the Corsair was characterized by its long-nosed fuselage and inverted gull-wing design. This fighter was plagued by a series of teething problems that prevented it from being deployed in any great numbers until 1943 in spite of its prewar design. The F4U was initially designed as a carrier fighter to serve on the new Essex-class carriers that were being built at the time. The Navy deemed the Corsair too unstable in its landing characteristics to be an ideal carrier fighter; it had a tendency to blow tires and make high bounces upon touchdown. Eventually of course the problems were ironed out, but not until the Corsair had been relegated to land service amongst both the naval and marine squadrons that were flying them.

The Corsair served throughout the island campaigns of 1943 and 1944, proving to be more than a match for all the Japanese planes that it encountered. Most of the pilots that flew the Corsair found it to be the best combat aircraft that the Navy flew in World War II, even better than the F6F Hellcat. Its major flaw was that the Corsair could be an unforgiving aircraft to new pilots, but in the hands of a master it was deadly to its enemies. The Corsair was known by a wide variety of nicknames during the course of its long service life, everything from "whistling death" (by the Japanese) to "the bent wing ensign eliminator" (by training instructors).

The Douglas SBD Dauntless

At the war's beginning the US Navy had perfected the tactic of dive-bombing to overcome the lack of carrying capability of ship-borne attack aircraft. The Douglas SBD (known as "slow but deadly") was the epitome of the dive-bomber. Stable, and with a good carrying capability and range, the SBD was the weapon platform that won the battle of Midway for the US Navy by sinking four Japanese aircraft carriers.

The one complaint against the SBD was that it was slow (maximum speed 250 mph). Because of this, coordination between the different portions of the Fleet aircraft was difficult. The fighters, being much faster than the SBDs, had to fly "S" curve patterns in order to keep with their bomber charges. Because the fighters had a smaller operational radius this slow speed of the SBD limited the range at which the US Fleet could deliver attacks. Coupled with this was the fact that the SBD did not have folding wings, which made storage of the aircraft difficult. The obvious answer for the Navy was to design an aircraft that had similar range as the SBD but increased speed and carrying capacity, and folding wings.

The Curtiss SB2C Helldiver

Even before the war the Navy was aware of the design limitations of the SBD. The Dauntless was simply too slow to accomplish the mission that the Navy wished of its dive-bombers. Therefore, in 1939, the Navy contracted with the Curtiss aircraft company to produce a new up-graded dive-bomber, the SB2C Helldiver. From the beginning the aircraft had difficulties: crashes and unstable handling characteristics plagued the Helldiver so much that several times the Navy almost cancelled the contract. Eventually an increased rudder size saved the project, and the SB2C was deployed with the Fleet in 1943.

Right from the beginning of its service the Helldiver was unpopular with the crew that had to fly it. Dubbed "the Beast," the SB2C had several undesirable handling characteristics, such as a high stall speed and an unfortunate tendency to dip its wings on final approach. At one point several prominent command officers recommended that the SB2C be removed from service in favor of the old tried and true SBD, but the same limitations that plagued the SBD were still present, and the Helldiver served to the end of the war.

The Douglas TBD Devastator

The Douglass TBD was the first all-metal low-wing aircraft to join the Navy. In 1937 this was the most advanced torpedo plane in the world. With its folding wings, the Devastator was a revolution in the design of carrier aircraft. However, the TBD was not destined to enjoy a long and distinguished career with the US Navy. Its demise was caused primarily by its lack of performance, a dismal 200 mph, and a range of only 700 miles.

The Grumman TBF Avenger

The Avenger design came about through the Navy's need for an attack aircraft with improved performance capabilities over the Dauntless and the Devastator. Grumman, long know in the Navy as the "iron works" because of its rugged designs, submitted the Avenger to the Navy in 1940 and had the aircraft delivered in 1941. The difference between the Avenger and other naval carrier aircraft was its immense size. With a wing span of 54 feet, a length of 42 feet, and a weight of over 15,000 lb, the Avenger was the largest carrier plane in the world.

In spite of its huge size the TBF was an improvement over the Devastator. The Avenger was faster by 78 mph and had a far greater range at over 900 miles. The bomb load was also greater, weighing in at an impressive 2,000 lb as compared to the 1,200 lb of the TBD. One feature that the Devastator and the Avenger shared was the abysmal performance of the Mk. XIII torpedo. Until this erratic weapon was improved the Avenger was used primarily as a glide or horizontal bomber, which limited its effectiveness against Japanese warships.

THE WEAPONS OF THE NAVAL AVIATOR

Machine guns

At the start of the war the United States Navy had two excellent machine guns, the .30 caliber M1919MA4 (AN-M2) and the .50 caliber M1921M2. Both were manufactured in the United States in versions designed for both land and air combat and were carried on virtually all US Navy aircraft. In 1941 the typical USN fighter plane was armed with four .50 caliber Browning M2 heavy machine guns. These highly successful weapons had already proved their worth in action all over the world. But if the weapons were adequate for the job ahead, the aircraft were not. The Navy's F2A Buffalo fighters had been of sound design before the war, but by 1941 they were hopelessly obsolete. Other fighterplane designs were already planned, but it would take time for them to be produced in numbers.

In contrast to the Buffalo, the Grumman F4F Wildcat was a promising design. Although armed only with four .50 caliber guns and without folding wings as yet, the Wildcat was still a sturdy, heavily armored and reliable fighter. But it too had flaws in its design: the loading of the ammunition for the machine guns was far from perfect, causing jamming in battle. Pre-war testing of the gun systems by the Navy VF squadrons was always per- formed at far less than the

The US Navy continued to experiment with air-launched rockets throughout the war. Shown here mounted on the wing rails of a TBM "Avenger" are the 3.5 in. ARs. In this photograph Navy deck crew attempt to keep the TBM from going over the side of the ship. (National Archives)

aircraft's full capacity for ammunition and under less than realistic combat maneuvering conditions. In combat, high G maneuvers would cause the ammo belts on the early production F4Fs to kink, resulting in a jam. This was a serious problem for the wing-mounted M1921M2 in combat throughout the first year of the war.

The M2 Browning was not the only machine gun utilized by the US Navy on carrier-based attack aircraft; both dive and torpedo bombers were armed with twin .30 caliber Browning M1919 machine guns. Mounted in the rear fuselage, these guns comprised the sole defensive armament for these slow-flying aircraft. By and large in the first year and a half of the war they proved little more than a nuisance to attacking Japanese aircraft, entirely useless for any but direct stern attacks. By the end of the war, however, the armament of these aircraft had been increased to two .50 caliber M2 machine guns, which gave the SBDs and TBFs a good chance to defend themselves against enemy attack.

Rockets

As the war progressed, it was found that fighters could be more effective in close support of ground troops if they were armed with rockets, in conjunction with their normal array of heavy machine guns and wing cannons. Originally designed by the British for use against German U-boats, these first air-to-surface weapons were 3.5 in. in diameter and carried a solid warhead.

Aviation ordnance man Paul Hoff was one of the first Americans trained in the use of the new weapons aboard the USS *Block Island* (CVE 21) in the Atlantic:

> Being the youngest second class in the ordnance gang I was given the job of handling the 3.5s. I think that all the older guys would rather load bombs and machine guns, they (other ordnance men) didn't like them because they were new weapons.

Yet in spite of the new and untried status of these weapons, the 3.5 AR (air rocket) proved to be a safe and effective weapon in the war against the U-boat. Unlike conventional depth charges, the 3.5 in. rockets gave the pilots of the TBF/Ms a piece of ordnance with the ability to strike U-boats directly.

The next generation of ARs saw the standard 3.5 in. rocket motor

By the war's end the US Navy had developed a 5in. high velocity HVAR rocket known as "Holy Moses" to aid the Marines in the role of close air support. This weapon was also used in an anti-shipping role against Japanese naval targets. (National Archives)

married to a 5 in. dual-purpose naval shell. The result was a weapon that was more effective against surface targets than the earlier 3.5 in. rocket, but with far less velocity and range. This lack of range and velocity was solved when the US Navy introduced one of the most successful of all air-to-surface rockets, the High Velocity Air Rocket, HVAR-5.

These 5 in. rockets could be launched from a variety of aircraft including the F6F Hellcat, the F4U Corsair, and the TBF/M Avenger. One problem, however, was the use of a rail-launch system for the 3.5 in. AR. These rocket rails caused excessive drag on the aircraft in flight, effectively limiting the employment of rockets to the TBF/Ms. With the development of the HVAR-5 rocket a new limited drag, zero friction hard point was introduced. The practical results of the change would not only increase the velocity of the rockets but also allow them to be mounted on the sleeker, higher performance Navy fighters.

During the campaign to take the island of Okinawa, USN and USMC rocket-armed fighter bombers launched accurate air strikes against Japanese positions within 100 yards of the American front lines, greatly increasing the effectiveness of the ground attacks.

The HVAR, however, was not particularly useful against heavily armored fighting vessels. In response, the US Navy developed a large 11.75 in. attack rocket called the "Tiny Tim." This huge weapon proved to be a failure because it could not be launched from hard points due to its large size. Moreover it had to free-fall before its engine would ignite, making the rocket very inaccurate.

Taboo in the modern US Navy, this ordnance crew load their "love" message, a 1,000 lb bomb, into the bomb bay of a TBM. (National Archives)

An unfortunate incident in the history of the 11.75 in. rocket occurred in 1945 aboard the USS *Franklin* off the coast of Okinawa during a Japanese air attack. A member of the crew, Lt. Cdr. Samuel R. Sherman, MD, was on hand to report the effects:

> I saw the Japanese plane coming in, but there was nothing I could do but stay there and take it. The plane just flew right in and dropped two bombs on our flight deck. I was blown about 15 feet into the air and tossed against the steel bulkhead of the island. I got up groggily and saw an enormous fire. All those planes that were lined up to take off were fully armed and fueled. The dive-bombers were equipped with this new "Tiny Tim" heavy rocket and they immediately began to explode. Some of the rockets' motors ignited and took off across the flight deck on their own. A lot of us were just ducking those things. It was pandemonium and chaos for hours and hours.[7]

Bombs, Depth Charges, and Torpedoes

The United States Navy had played a leading role in the development of air-launched ordnance such as torpedoes and depth charges in the years leading up to World War I. During the interwar decades, in a climate of pacifism and arms limitations, the Navy lagged behind the other maritime nations of the world in the development of new antishipping ordnance. Most of the shortcomings of ordnance in the early years of the war were a direct result of poor design.

A fine study of a fighter pilot prior to his flight in his F6F "Hellcat". Of note is the metal plotting board and navigational compass. (National Archives)

Furthermore, prior to the beginning of World War II, interservice rivalries had led to the development of two different and incompatible sets of bombs, one for the Navy and one for the Army. In the late 1930s this situation was remedied by the introduction of a joint service standard bomb, which, with certain variations, could be used by both Army and Navy aircraft. The primary difference between the two was the fuses: the Army variant was often armed as soon as it was released from the bomb rack, while the Navy version had a timed delay mechanism as a safety precaution for carrier operations.

In addition to the A/N bomb the Navy also maintained a number of special types of armor-piercing bombs in the 1,000 lb range that were specifically designed with delayed action fuses allowing them to penetrate a target's armor prior to exploding. It was with these weapons that the SBD-2 and -3 "Dauntless" dive-bombers of VB-6 scored the two hits that sank the Japanese carrier *Akagi* at the battle of Midway.

One area of severe deficiency in the early war period was in the torpedoes with which the Fleet was armed. The Bliss-Leavitt Mk. 13, 14, and 15 torpedoes had several difficulties that needed to be overcome. Discussion will be limited to the Mk. 13, since the Mk.

14 and 15 were not air-launched weapons.

The Mk. 13 was a product of the postwar experimentation that the Navy conducted during the 1920s. The Mk. 13 was a flawed weapon system for a variety of reasons. Since it was too heavy (2,216 lb/1,005 kg) to be carried by the biplane bombers of the early 1930s, the Mk. 13 never received realistic combat testing. It was also a relatively short weapon (13 ft 5 in.), making it unstable compared to the highly effective Japanese Type 94 "Long Lance" Torpedo. The Mk. 13's design demanded that the approach run to the target be made at a speed of less than 90 knots and at an altitude of less than 100 feet. Even under ideal conditions the Mk. 13 was notorious for diving deep upon launch (sounding) or breaking up on contact with the water. If this catalog of woes were not enough, the Mk. 13 was a slow weapon, able to reach speeds of only 33 knots, requiring extreme skill or luck to score hits on swift Japanese ships.

The carrier battles of 1942 had shown that the command of a task force was a demanding job on the admiral in charge of the Fleet. By 1944 the Americans had developed a system of command rotation whereby Admirals Mitscher and Halsey alternated command of the American Fleet. Here Mitscher and his chief of staff, A. A. "Thirty Knot" Burke, plan some of the operations off Okinawa in June of 1945. (National Archives)

Eventually most of the problems with the Mk. 13 were corrected by the simple expedient of attaching a wooden drag device to the weapon's nose and a set of boxes to the tailfin to increase the stability and slow the speed of the torpedo as it entered the water. The wooden attachments would then break off and the weapon could run as normal.

Real torpedo improvement came with the introduction of the Mk. 24 acoustic homing torpedo, nicknamed "FIDO" because it would track a target like a bloodhound. Designed to counter the Axis submarine threat, the Mk. 24 was a miracle of wartime design necessity, having made the transition from initial design to Fleet introduction in a little less than 18 months. The Navy's specification called for a weapon that could fit the standard aircraft 1,000 lb bomb rack and could be dropped from a height of 200 feet at a speed of up to 120 knots.

FIDO was equipped with hydrophones, which steered it toward the target by homing in on the source of the strongest sound signals in its vicinity. FIDO was also equipped with a device that was designed to protect friendly vessels, by turning off the acoustic homing device if the Mk. 24 rose too close to the surface. Even so, FIDO had difficulty in distinguishing between the sounds of Allied surface ships and of Axis submarines. As a consequence, the Mk. 24 was rarely used in conjunction with friendly surface vessels in ASW operations.

THE CARRIER WAR, 1941–45: AIR TACTICS

Assigned to the air group, the pilots aboard an aircraft carrier numbered only 100 out of the total ship's complement of men. Yet they were the reason for the existence of the ship. The organization of the air group was simple: the headman was the Commander, Air Group (CAG), who was usually either a full commander or lieutenant commander. Under the air group commander circa 1942 were three squadrons totaling 75 aircraft: 21 F4F-4 Wildcat fighters, 36 SBD-3 Dauntless dive-bombers, and 18 TBD Devastator torpedo bombers. The squadrons were commanded by a lieutenant commander or a full lieutenant, and were divided into three divisions commanded by the squadron commander, the executive officer and the flight officer respectively.

An early 1945 picture showing two pilots from USS *Hornet* CV-9. Of note is the metal plotting board held by the figure on the left. (National Archives)

These divisions were further sub-divided into two plane sections commanded by the most experienced aviator irrespective of his rank. As the war went on the exact makeup of the air group and the number of planes in each respective squadron would change in accordance with the exact circumstances of battle and the nature of the foe that was encountered. For example, by 1945, when the threat from Japanese surface forces had decreased and the kamikaze attack was in full swing, the number of fighters in the air groups was increased to 36 to counter the threat posed by these difficult targets.

The fighters

The basic element of the fighter squadron was the section of three planes, the leader, and his two wingmen. US Navy prewar doctrine for fighter tactics stressed the necessity of maintaining tight formation and cooperation between all parts of a section. The section formed up in a tight V formation with a man on either wing of the leader. The section leader was to initiate all maneuvers, and the wingmen were to keep close station. The basic concept was developed before there was good radio contact amongst aircraft, and the formation allowed the leader to keep visual contact with his section. The main disadvantage of the formation was its rigidity and the inconvenience to the section leader, who was obliged to look constantly from side to side to see if his wingmen were on station. This constant head swiveling took too much of a section leader's time and forced him to worry about the details of the formation when he needed to be watching for enemy aircraft. Some section leaders felt that they needed three eyes to keep track of their unwieldy formations.

The US Naval Aviator – Uniform and Equipment

A

Lieutenant Thatch's "Beam Defense"

1

2

3

4

5

6

B

Attack of the VB–6 on *Hiryu* – Battle of Midway

c

D

Landing of an F6F

E

F

Changes began to appear in the arena of fighter tactics as evidenced by the authorization in 1940 for experimentation with two plane sections by fighter squadrons VF-2 and VF-5. The changes were found to improve pilot visibility while at the same time reducing the amount of time necessary for the section to form up with other sections of the division. Initially there was opposition to these changes from Admiral William Halsey, who felt that the improvements over the current system were only minimal. VF-2 and VF-5 were allowed to continue with the experimentation with the smaller sections. By the summer of 1941, after reviewing the data from the air war in Europe and China where the tight three-plane formations were found to be ineffective, all the fighter squadrons of the US Navy were reorganized into three divisions of six planes each, with each division consisting of three two-plane sections.

When the war began for America the fighter squadrons had been undergoing a renaissance in both tactics and organization for the best part of a year. American leaders like Admiral King and Admiral Halsey were overseeing the necessary changes to the aviation service. The Japanese attack at Pearl Harbor, like the British attack on the Italian Fleet at Taranto in 1940, had shown to the world the vulnerability of capital ships to air attack. From the winter of 1941 to the spring of 1943 the ships and aircraft of the aviation service, along with the submarine forces, would be the only US forces holding the Pacific line against the wave of Japanese conquest.

The carrier versus carrier battles of Coral Sea, Midway, and Guadalcanal in 1942 taught the aviation leaders of the US Navy many valuable lessons in both tactics and doctrine. While the tide of Japanese victory had been stemmed at Coral Sea and Midway, the cost had been heavy, with two American Fleet carriers, USS *Lexington* and USS *Yorktown*, being sunk. These heavy losses would be further aggravated during the Guadalcanal campaign, especially in the battle of the eastern Solomons and Santa Cruz Island, with the loss of USS *Wasp* and USS *Hornet* respectively. At one point in October of 1942, following the battle of Santa Cruz Island, America would have only one carrier, the USS *Enterprise* (damaged), in operation in the Pacific theater.

The chief lesson that was learned during the 1942 campaign was the need for more fighters. An American naval aviator flying a fighter plane could find himself engaged in a wide variety of missions. Air operations leaned heavily on the VF squadrons, with daily Combat Air Patrols (CAP) as well as escorts for all the attack squadrons of a strike mission. During this particular year the American carriers had onboard only one squadron of fighters each, approximately 27 aircraft. Operational losses associated with these hazardous missions caused the number of available aircraft to dwindle very quickly. For example, at the battle of the Coral Sea Admiral Fletcher's Task Force 17 consisted of two aircraft carriers, USS *Lexington* and USS *Yorktown*. Between the two ships they fielded only 30-odd fighters due to mechanical failures and losses in previous actions. At several key points in 1942 during the battles of the Coral Sea and Midway, there were just not enough fighters to go around. The results were quite predictable: unescorted strike missions took heavy losses and weak CAPs were unable to stem Japanese air assaults.

One other difficulty was in the area of air group command-and-control, both human and radar. American carriers had started the war with fairly sophisticated air and surface search radar sets but this was not an unmixed blessing. While aircraft could be detected at far greater distances than by visual observation, not all American aircraft were equipped with Identify Friend or Foe (IFF) radar beacons, a simple device that emitted a preset signal pulse when detected by American radar. This lack of equipment led to much confusion since without the IFF device it was impossible to tell a friendly aircraft from a hostile one. The result was that CAP fighters often vectored in the wrong direction to intercept returning American aircraft misidentified as Bogeys (enemy aircraft) by the radar officer, leaving the carrier under-protected.

Indeed, as battle results would show, 1942 was a learning year for American commanders; control and coordination of air group attacks were a particular weak point in American combat operations. At Midway, for example, many of the USS

A fine study of USS *Yorktown* CV-10 pilots in August 1943 planning the approach to Marcus Island. This air strike was the first combat use of the F6F and the debut of the Essex- and Independence-class carriers. (National Archives)

Hornet's air group had to ditch at sea for want of gas, due to the poor planning of the commander of the *Hornet*'s air group. 1942 would also teach US naval planners the need for calm clear-thinking Fighter Direction Officers (FDOs).

The FDO's role was to vector the CAP to intercept any incoming enemy aircraft. The FDO was located in the ship's combat information center (CIC) where he would be in constant touch with both the aircraft of the combat air patrol and the ship's air search radar. Being the FDO was a demanding job that required an individual to make well-reasoned decisions about the allocation of the correct number of fighters to counter an enemy strike and still maintain an adequate reserve over his own flight decks. The FDOs had not been up to the task in 1942 at Coral Sea and Midway because of their lack of experience in combat situations and a still incomplete understanding of the capabilities and limitations of the radar systems available to them.

One fortunate event that occurred for Naval intelligence was the capture of an almost intact A6M2 "Zero" fighter from the Aleutian Islands in 1942. This aircraft had been lost on a June raid of Dutch Harbor when the pilot attempted a rough field emergency landing after his aircraft was damaged in the raid. The aircraft flipped onto its back during the landing, killing its pilot. It was later discovered and salvaged by Navy aeronautical experts. Following the rebuilding of the Japanese fighter at NAS North Island, it was used in the training of new naval aviators, giving them some idea of the strengths and weaknesses of this hitherto mysterious enemy fighter. This use of captured aircraft for evaluation and training purposes recalls today's "Top Gun" school, and provides an example of the innovative use of resources by naval personnel.

The year 1943 was to be one of rebuilding, the costly carrier battles of 1942 having taught the US Navy aviators valuable lessons regarding their Japanese opponents. Far from being the incompetents they were thought to have been before the war, Japanese Navy pilots had revealed themselves to be very capable indeed, particularly in their willingness to press home attacks against heavily defended targets. The question remained, could America overcome the disadvantages inflicted by the raid on Pearl Harbor to achieve victory or would a negotiated peace with Japan be the best America could do?

The arrival of the new Fleet carriers, beginning with USS *Essex* on the last day of 1942, began to ease the problems of numbers of ships that had plagued US Navy operational planners. Ship designers back in the US took into consideration as many lessons of carrier air operations in their design of the new Essex class. First, the new ships had three deck elevators and two forward catapults to speed up air operations, allowing the decks of the ship to be cleared rapidly during action. Each of the Essex-class vessels was larger then the previous class of carriers by some 60 feet and had enlarged hangar decks in order to allow for the increased complement of aircraft. From the prewar number of 18 fighters, the VF squadrons were enlarged to 36 aircraft in 1943.

One lesson that had been learned during the naval operations of the Guadalcanal campaign was the need for coordinated close air support for ground forces. At Guadalcanal the carriers were only on station for the first two days of the operation, and significant numbers of land-based aircraft were not available to the ground commander until later in the month of August. This lack of aircraft meant that the US forces on Guadalcanal were hampered from interdicting the flow of Japanese reinforcements to the island and was one of the reasons for the difficulties for the Marine landing division. This situation was remedied by improved coordination between air support and ground forces by the addition of specially trained naval personnel who went in with the ground forces to evaluate air-support needs and call in the right number and kind of aircraft for the mission. Command in control was further improved in 1944 by the addition of special "command ships" designed with improved radar and radio control equipment that allowed for the smooth control of naval air support over the invasion beachheads.

As American invasion forces moved closer to the Japanese home islands, the defenders became ever more fierce and desperate. During the Philippine invasion the Japanese unveiled their most desperate gamble of all, the kamikaze. The situation that the Japanese were facing in 1944–45 was daunting: American carrier forces in the Pacific had grown to 31 ships with over 1,000 aircraft on their combined flight decks. In order to deal with the kamikaze threat new tactics were developed by (now Commander) Jimmy Thatch. The usual American procedure had been to launch a deck load air strike that consisted of about half the carrier's air group at a particular target. Half the planes made the initial strike and then returned; the other half of the group would then proceed with the second strike. The main problem with this system was the amount of time it took to launch and recover planes. Commander Thatch's plan called for constant air raids over Japanese-held airfields, and in order to achieve this he introduced what he called a "three strike" system. Later nicknamed "The Big Blue Blanket," Thatch's plan was to divide the carrier air group into three smaller sections. These would take less time to launch and recover, thereby allowing for greater time over the enemy airfields. Thatch's plan was to make regular fighter sweeps of the Japanese bases to keep the enemy forces tied down in defensive struggles over their own fields rather than allowing them to make offensive raids on the American forces.

As a further precaution, the American commanders needed to take steps to improve their early warning system. Thus a plan was developed involving an extended CAP of eight fighters called "tom cats" to cover a barrier of picket ships, called "watchdogs," equipped with radar approximately 50 miles from the invasion beaches. This barrier patrol would fly racetrack courses over the picket ships in areas where returning American air strikes were expected. At this barrier the returning American strike forces were inspected or "deloused" for enemy aircraft that might be trailing them back to the US Fleet. In addition to these mandatory check points, Cdr. Thatch established "no fly" zones, in which all aircraft were to be viewed as fair game and free for shooting at. These practical solutions eased the problems that radar operators were encountering with screen clutter, and made the job of the fighter direction officer easier.

Each of the "watchdog" picket ships also carried a trained fighter direction officer (FDO) who was in constant communication with the command ship closer to the invasion anchorage. Under the direction of the FDO, fighter CAPs could be vectored toward approaching enemy aircraft long before the kamikazes were in range of the American carriers. In testimony to the effectiveness of this defensive tactic, the Japanese began to attack the picket vessels in order to destroy the US Navy's early warning capability. During the 88-day Okinawa campaign, the Japanese launched nearly 900 air raids with a total of over 3,000 aircraft. Of these the CAP shot down over 1,000. The success of the American tactic was not without cost to the defenders, however; seven American destroyers were sunk, 18 seriously damaged, and six lightly damaged.

Okinawa was the largest amphibious operation of the entire Pacific War and it was here that the US Navy's ability to project sea power could be seen at its highest level. During the 88 days of the campaign Navy and Marine aircraft flew 1,900 ground attack sorties and over 17,000 sorties of all kinds. The Navy maintained over 500 aircraft aloft on a daily basis, and overall they expended 9,000,000 rounds of .50 caliber ammunition, 49,000 5 in. rockets, over 7,000 lb of bombs, and 200,000 gallons of napalm on Japanese targets.

The night fighters

One of the many innovations of the United States Navy in World War II was the introduction of shipborne night fighters for the protection of the Fleet. When America began its drive across the central Pacific in 1943, Japanese forces operating from land bases began a series of night

As the war progressed the need for night fighters became more and more important. These F4U-2s have been equipped with Army-Navy standard alternating pulse radar AN/APS-4 mounted on the right wing. They are flying from the USS *Intrepid* CV 11 in February 1944. (National Archives)

air raids against the aircraft carriers. These raids were difficult to stop because of the lack of training among the air groups in night takeoffs and landings. Even antiaircraft fire proved to be a mixed blessing because attacking Japanese aircraft could use the muzzle flashes to locate the American Fleet.

What was needed to counter these attacks was an entirely different approach to fleet defense, the radar-guided night fighter. The first of these aircraft was the F6F-3 "Hellcat," already in use as the standard Navy day fighter. The Hellcats were to operate in pairs teamed with the radar-equipped TBF/(M) Avenger. At best this was a cumbersome system; the plan called for the fighters and the torpedo bombers to be vectored toward any radar contacts by the ship's fighter direction officer. Once the aircraft were within 10–15 miles of the "bogey," direction of the operation would then pass to the radar operator on board the TBF, who would then direct the Hellcats to within visual range of the target. The practical difficulties of target identification in this type of operation were apparent from the outset when the originator of the plan, Lt. Cdr. Butch O'Hare, was killed on one of the first night intercept missions.

Subsequent missions would show the need for improved air-search radar to be carried by the fighters themselves. The first of these radar units was mounted under the wing. The device was an improvement over those initially used by the TBFs, yet the drag that the unit created on the F6F-3N disturbed the handling of the aircraft and made the fighter difficult to land on carrier decks. By 1944 the fighters were so improved that it was common practice among the air groups to fly a night CAP. The night fighters were launched into the darkness in order to ensure the safety and security of the Fleet by keeping its presence undetected by enemy aircraft. These night launches were harrowing experiences for the aircrews, accomplished by means of a hydraulic catapult located on the bow of the carrier:

> The worst thing of it [the catapult launch] is thinking about it beforehand. You always wish you didn't have to do it, but the idea is worse than the real thing. When they pull that trigger, you get the most horrible damn sensation in the world. It isn't pain at all. It just goes all over you and you've got to scream, but before you can get the scream out the whole thing is over and you are flying.[8]

The lessons learned by the night fighters in 1943–44 would be incorporated into the new versions of naval aircraft, the F6F-5N, F4U-2N, and the TBM-3N. The two fighters were equipped with improved air-search radar, the Army-Navy, Air Pulse Search (AN/APS-4), that allowed the radar operator to pick up contacts at a range of five miles. The TBM-3D was even equipped with an early form of radar jamming device that was useful in night raids to disrupt Japanese search radars.

The dive-bombers

The summer of 1941 saw American naval forces flying the Douglas SBD "Dauntless." This aircraft was the first purpose-built dive-bomber since the inception of the tactic by the US Marine Corps in the 1920s and served in large numbers with American Fleet bombing squadrons.

The "push over." These SBDs are at the point of beginning their 70° angle dive-bombing run on their target. Attacks of this nature need to be made from a high altitude in order to allow time for the pilots to pull their plane out (October 1942). (National Archives)

By 1941 bombing tactics were well established in the naval aviation community. US naval doctrine divided attacks into two basic categories, glide and dive-bombing. The primary difference between the two was the altitude at which the attack was made and the angle at which the bombs were delivered. The Navy termed any attack delivered at less than 8,000 feet and at less than a 70° angle of dive to be a glide bombing attack, "For daylight attacks on well-defended combatant ships the following is true: As the angle of dive decreases from the optimum (70°) the percentage of hits decreases and damage to your own plane increases."[9]

Bombing attacks were divided into three distinct phases: the approach, the delivery, and the withdrawal. Naval aviators were taught to approach their target at high altitude, over 15,000 feet. Doctrine throughout the war stated that the additional visibility gained by this greater altitude would offset any disadvantages suffered by the attacking group from early detection by enemy radar. Once the dive-bombers had reached their initial point (IP), about ten miles from the target, they would split up in order to attack the target from several angles. Dives on the target began from an altitude of 15,000 to 17,000 feet at an angle of 70°. The "push-over" occurred when the dive-bombers began their descent on the targets; at this point the SBDs deployed special dive brakes to prevent air compression on the control surfaces of their planes. Once the Dauntless reached 2,500 feet the bomb would be released and the pullout would begin. When the dive-bombers reached mast-level altitude they would begin a low-level withdrawal from the target, jinking (making small changes in altitude and course) until they were out of range of the antiaircraft fire. According to Lt. Cdr. William O. Burch of VS-5 of USS *Yorktown*, American pilots were skillful at the aiming process, "Our sight are set that, in a 70-degree dive, you put your pipper [aim point] right on the target, without any wind. With practice, you get so you can judge pretty close what angle you are diving at."[10]

The early SBDs relied on a telescopic sight to aim their bombs. During numerous early actions in the Pacific it was found that these sights would fog up as the planes passed from the cold air of high altitude to the much warmer air at lower altitudes. The resulting fogging was a great factor in their disappointing showing in the battles of 1942. Not until the arrival of the SBD-5 and the Curtiss SB2C "Hell Diver" in 1943–44 was the sighting problem completely solved by the replacement of the telescopic sight with a more reliable reflector-type sight.

The torpedo bombers

It is difficult to find a sadder or more ironic story of World War II combat than that of the men who flew the early US Navy torpedo planes. Brave young pilots and their crews were committed to flying obsolete aircraft armed with a virtually useless torpedo. Yet the irony lies in the fact that from the end of World War I and throughout the 1920s the US Navy led the world in the development of air-launched torpedoes and the tactics of their delivery.

Beginning in 1934 the Bureau of Aeronautics (BuAer) called for the design of a new torpedo bomber to replace the biplanes then currently serving with the Fleet. The resulting winner of the contract competition was the Douglas Devastator (TBD). Combining many innovations in design, such as folding wings for easy storage on carriers and an all-metal

Pilots beginning to man their planes aboard USS *Saratoga* prior to a strike. These pilots wear the standard Navy flight dress. Note the mixture of footwear: both shoes and ankle boots. (National Archives)

construction, the TBD was a very advanced craft for the time. Unfortunately the increasing demands of war rendered the TBD obsolete by 1942.

The final and fatal difficulty with the TBD was its weapon, the Bliss-Leavitt Mk. 13 aerial torpedo. The Mk. 13 was a flawed weapon; if it did not break up on impact with the water, it was prone to run too deep in the water, often passing completely under the target ship. In order to lessen the impact of the water, the TBD had to fly "low and slow," releasing the torpedo at less than 90 knots and under 100 feet in altitude.

From a tactical standpoint the American doctrine was fairly sound and standard, being divided again into approach, attack, and withdrawal. One prewar concept that was found to be impractical under battle conditions was the use of aircraft (smokers) to lay smoke curtains in front of the oncoming TBDs. The smoker was to fly parallel to the course of the target, laying down a curtain of smoke from a wing-mounted generator. The remainder of the squadron then fanned out to deliver an attack on both the port and starboard bow of the target ship simultaneously; this was the classic "anvil" attack. This attack, if properly delivered, would guarantee hits on the ship, for no matter which way she turned the target vessel would place itself squarely in the path of the oncoming torpedoes.

The most successful example of a simultaneous port and starboard attack against a warship occurred at the battle of the Coral Sea in 1942 when Devastators of VT-2 flying off the USS *Lexington* sank the Japanese aircraft carrier *Shoho*.

The operational difficulties that plagued the Mk. 13 system and the weakness of the Douglas Devastator in the face of fighter attack served to bring the usefulness of the torpedo attack into doubt. It was not until design modifications were made to the Mk. 13 torpedo and the introduction of a new torpedo bomber, the Grumman TBF/ TBM Avenger, later in the war, that the US Navy would again feel confident in its ability to launch successful torpedo attacks on Japanese naval vessels.

The VT squadrons were at last vindicated in their adherence to American torpedo tactics when in 1944 at the battle of Leyte Gulf American aircrews sank the Japanese super battleship *Musashi*. In a classic combined high-low attack made in conjunction with dive-bombers the Avengers were able to make a high-speed approach against the *Musashi* and her escorts. As the American VT squadrons moved in for the kill the

Japanese gunners attempted to knock down the American aircraft with gunfire directed into the ocean directly in the flight path of the oncoming Americans. The commanding officer of VT-13, Cdr. Larry French, flying off the USS *Franklin*, described the action: "These salvos were ineffective against the torpedo attack, as we were approaching the release point at about 260 knots and 600–800 ft."[11]

The results of the attack were highly successful as the VTs scored 19 hits on the *Musashi* that contributed to its sinking.

Patrol and Observation Squadrons

The Navy started World War II with two types of specialty squadrons, dedicated to patrol (VP) and observation (VO) respectively. In the Pacific the duties of these two squadrons were increasingly taken over by the carrier air groups themselves, but this was not the case in the Atlantic convoy environment.

In the Atlantic the VP squadrons, in conjunction with the crews of the lighter-than-air blimp squadrons, were responsible primarily for escorting convoys and other antisubmarine patrol missions. Operating from bases as far south as Brazil and as north as Iceland, the aviators and aircrews of the VP and the VPB (patrol bombing) squadrons did much to close the so-called "Black Gap" in the Atlantic Ocean. This was the area where U-boats had hitherto been able to operate with little or no interference from Allied aircraft. With the increased availability of long-range patrol planes, such as the PB4Y-1 "Liberator" in 1943 and the PB4Y-2 "Privateer" in 1944, the US Navy helped to close this gap, strategically sealing the fate of the German U-boat effort.

As the war in the Pacific progressed, both the patrol (VP) and cruiser observation (VO) squadrons were called upon to perform more and more search and rescue flights for Allied fliers, known as "Dumbo" missions. Commonly the VP squadrons were equipped with amphibians, like the PBY "Catalina" and the PB4Y-1 Martin Mariner. Operating from primitive forward bases like Guadalcanal and Tulagi, this duty was difficult and unsung, but during the course of the war in the central and south Pacific PBYs amassed a fine record in the rescue of downed US fliers.

Early in the war the US Navy converted seven light cruiser hulls under construction into the CVLs of the USS Independence class. This photograph of an F6F "Hellcat" on the forward elevator shows the close quarters on the flight decks on the small carriers (1944). (National Archives)

During the Okinawa campaign one six-plane section of Martin Mariners made 76 water landings, rescuing 183 downed American aviators. In 1945 alone the VP "Dumbo" missions were responsible for the rescue of over 2,000 flight personnel of all services. The success of these air-sea rescue missions helped to keep the moral of American air groups high and increased the likelihood of maximum efforts on their part. It was a great comfort to the combat pilots to be assured that the Navy would make every effort to save them if they were shot down.

One major innovation in aircraft design that improved the effectiveness of the Mariners on "Dumbo" missions was the introduction of jet-assisted take off (JATO) during the Iwo Jima campaign. The Navy's Martin Mariners were equipped with rocket packs that decreased the time and space necessary for the take off of the large flying boats. The practical result of this invention was to give the rescue squadrons the ability to land close to enemy-held positions, effect a rescue, and get out of the area as quickly as possible. Many aviators who might otherwise have been killed or captured were now being rescued to fight another day.

The role of the patrol squadrons was not restricted to peaceful search and rescue missions. The need for night interdiction missions was made clear by Japanese operations in and around Guadalcanal in 1942. Correctly fearing the strike power of the US Marine squadrons at Henderson Field, the Japanese decided on nighttime resupply missions for their troops on "the Canal" by sea. The traffic generated by these missions was so great that it was termed the "Tokyo Express." In order to counteract this, the Navy needed to develop a night bombing capability, and the mission fell to the PBY squadrons operating in the south Pacific.

Deployed for evaluation by Admiral Aubrey Fitch, VP-12, the first "Black Cat" squadron, arrived at Henderson Field on Guadalcanal in December 1942. The unit took its name from the combination of the non-reflective black paint of their PBYs and the name of the aircraft, "Catalina." The name "Black Cat" must have been a good omen, for, according to squadron legend, two days after VP-12 arrived at Henderson Field, a small black cat wandered out of the jungle and "adopted" the men of the squadron; in turn the men took the little cat as their mascot. The cat stayed with them until the squadron was due to rotate back to the United States, when it vanished just as mysteriously as it had appeared.

The success of VP-12 and the other night operations at this time was made possible by the development of the radar altimeter in the years just prior to World War II. This rather simple device bounced sound waves off the surface of the water back to the flying aircraft. By calculating the time necessary for the sound signal to return it was possible to determine accurately the altitude of the aircraft. For the "Black Cat" pilots the radar altimeter made the dangerous low-level night attacks on Japanese shipping possible.

Seldom mentioned but equally important to the Navy's war effort in the Pacific theater was the use of long-range patrol bombers to locate and interdict Japanese merchant shipping and to bomb land targets beyond the reach of carrier-based aircraft. Starting in 1944, the patrol bombing (VPB) squadrons operating from bases in the Philippines were able to make air raids deep into previously untouched Japanese-held Indo-China. Like their compatriots in the Atlantic, the VPBs of the Pacific were able to bring enemy merchant shipping to a virtual standstill before the war's end.

COMBAT AIR OPERATIONS, 1944–45

The US Pacific Fleet at the beginning of the 1944 was in fact two separate commands over the same ships: the Third Fleet under the command of Admiral Halsey and the Fifth Fleet under Admiral Spruance. Both Spruance and Halsey took turns with the command of the Fleet, and this allowed each command team time to rest from the stress of Fleet operations and gave them opportunities to plan their forthcoming campaigns. Each commander had his own separate command staff, including different task force commanders, Admirals McCain and Mitscher respectively. McCain and Mitscher were in overall tactical command of the Fleet; they were responsible for choosing where and when the attacks would be made.

Typical Wartime Strike Mission, 1944

Prior to any mission, the commander of the air group (CAG) and his squadron commanders began to study intelligence estimates of possible enemy air defenses, including antiaircraft artillery, fighter opposition, and search radar. Once an actual strike target was identified, several fighter sweeps, photo-reconnaissance missions, and night "heckler" flights would be flown in the target vicinity. The purpose of these missions was twofold: softening up enemy defenses and gathering information about the effectiveness of the Japanese search radar. The photographs from the reconnaissance missions were used along with any other information about the target to build detailed three-dimensional maps of the target area to aid in the planning of attack routes and ways of returning to the Fleet. After target selection, the senior flight operations officer would make the overall plan of the attack with help from the CAG of the flagship.

Once the basics of the plan were worked out, the squadron commanders would work on the actual details of the air strike. Fighter squadrons would assign aircraft to combat air patrol that would stay near the Fleet to protect the carriers in case of a counterstrike. Further VF units would also be assigned the role of bomber escort, flying either high cover or close support of the attack aircraft.

The types of ordnance and the method of the attack to be used by the VB squadrons were determined by the nature of the target. If, for example, the dive-bombers were to hit an airfield, a glide-bombing attack with a mixture of fragmentation bombs to destroy aircraft and heavy bombs to crater the runways would be used. Against shipping, armor or semi-armor-piercing bombs would be called for.

As soon as the night CAP landed, the plane handlers began to reposition the aircraft for the coming dawn attack. The flight deck officer had a six-foot model of

American naval aircraft such as this F6F Hellcat were of a radial engine design, which necessitated manual turning of the prop prior to starting the engine of the aircraft. (National Archives)

the carrier flight deck, called the "weejee board," on which he arranged models of all 48 planes to be launched on the strike. This deck plan would be carried out by the plane handlers in the darkness, who were aided only by the white lines marked on the deck and their familiarity with their aircraft.

Below the flight deck in the ordnance shack and the magazine the ordnance crew made final preparations to load the ordnance onto the aircraft. Early in the cruise extra bombs were sometimes stowed around the edges of the hangar deck not only for ease of loading but also to increase the number of bombs that the ship could carry. This extra ordnance would be the first to be loaded onto the aircraft since its presence in combat presented a very real hazard. Each ordnance crew had a specific job based on the nature of the strike; some would load bombs, some would belt the .50 caliber ammunition for the machine guns, while others would shuttle the ordnance from the magazine located deep inside the ship to the hangar deck.

The organized chaos of spotting planes for launch is clearly illustrated in this photograph. All crew members had to be constantly aware of the dangers of whirling propellers. (National Archives)

Elsewhere on the carrier the ship's cooks completed preparations for the air division's breakfast. The food served aboard a carrier was normally more than adequate, but on the days of big actions the cooks brought out the best, steak and eggs being a favorite among the pilots.

Shortly after reveille, the various crew members each took a moment to make personal preparations for battle. On the flight deck the planes stood gassed and armed. In the air plot, a small office above the flight deck in the island, the flight officer made his final preparations to launch the morning CAP. Down below decks the aircrews each went to their ready rooms to begin their briefings.

Saturday   July 10, 1944
Sunrise 0710   Duty Division-2nd
0340 Early Bird reveille on the bugle for the Air Department
0400 Early Breakfast for the Air Department
0445 Reveille all hands. Flight Quarters one blast
0505 Breakfast for the crew
0530 Breakfast in the Wardroom
0545 Launch Strike Able
0615 General Quarters

General Plan:
Strikes against the Japanese Air Bases at Saipan and Tinian of the Marianas Group will be continued though most of the day. Half group strikes, plus several special flights on photographic missions are scheduled. Operations permitting, the noon meal will be served on Battles Stations and the evening meal in the Mess hall.[12]

The ready rooms aboard the ship (each squadron had its own ready room) were crowded by the pilots who were to fly the first mission. Here the squadron commander and the air intelligence officer would brief the pilots. The details of the Fleet's present location, weather conditions, and the available information on the Fleet's location upon the pilot's return were passed around and copied by the pilots onto their plot boards.

The special considerations of the mission were also discussed by the squadron commanders, such as the location of the safe area for "Duds" or aircraft that for whatever reason could not complete the combat mission. Map coordinates of the rescue vessels for downed aircrews were given, along with the settings of the ship's homing beacon (YZ). At last the command "Pilots man your planes" was heard over the ship's intercom (squawk box), and the aircrews would begin to hustle out of the ready room onto the flight deck.

On the bridge of the carrier, the captain would inform the rest of the Fleet via the TBS (Talk Between Ships) set that air operations were about to begin. The signal flag "prep Fox" was hoisted to the dip of the signal yardarm, and the carrier turned into the wind and increased its speed prior to the launching of the aircraft. Near astern a destroyer would take up its assigned position as "plane guard" in case of any of the aircraft crashing upon launch.

Flight deck operations had proceeded apace. The plane captains of each aircraft had begun the process of starting all the engines with a device known as a "shotgun" starter. The device was operational when a blank cartridge was loaded into the breech of the starter. On the command "Stand by to start engines," the plane captain would prime the engine and turn on the magneto. After "Stand clear of propellers," followed shortly by "Start engines," the plane captain would fire the starter. The gas from the explosion forced the piston of the cylinder down and allowed the propeller to rotate. Soon the deck was blanketed by smoke and noise as the radial engines roared to full power.

The pilots would now quickly board their aircraft. The signal flag "Fox" was now hoisted to the top of the carrier yardarm and the first of the planes to be launched had its folding wings locked into flying position. The yellow-shirted plane handlers now began the carefully ordered launch procedure as the first plane taxied forward to the launch position. At this point the aviator was totally dependent upon the plane handlers, as his view of the ground was extremely limited from the cockpit of his big-engine aircraft.

Control of the plane was passed from one plane handler to another until the pilot taxied his plane to the launch position. The pilot now came under the direction of the chief plane handler, who ordered him to begin a full-power run up of the aircraft's

The SBD-5 in this 1944 photograph is on final full power prior to launch. The pilot has his eyes fixed on the aircraft handler and his checkered flag. When the handler drops the flag the pilot will release his brakes and launch the plane. (National Archives)

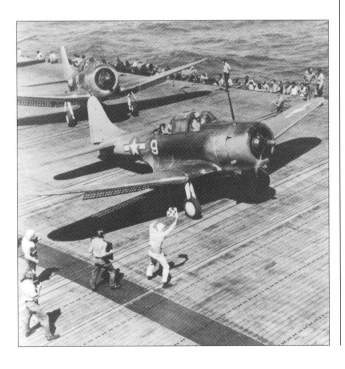

The alternative to the deck launch was a catapult launch. Here an SBD has just been catapulted into the air. (National Archives)

One of the most spectacular views, if rather scary, was the view from the rear seat of a TBF/M as it was launched from the deck. The carrier is the USS *Yorktown* CV 10, c.1944–45. (National Archives)

engine with the rapid twirling of his black and white checkered flag. If the engine checked out at full RPMs, the pilot signaled his readiness to launch with a "thumbs up" to the launch officer. The launch officer would drop his signal flag and point forward, the signal for launch, and the first aircraft of the strike rolled down the deck.

There were three different methods of departure for aircraft leaving on an air strike. An "urgent departure" called for sections of aircraft to make their way individually toward the target as soon as they were launched from the carrier. This method was only called for in case of an imminent attack by enemy forces. For example, the urgent departure method was used when the escort carriers of TAFFY 3 were attacked in the battle of Samar in October 1944.

"Normal departure" allowed for individual squadrons of aircraft to form up and make their own way to the target. Normal departure was used if the distance to the target called for some of the slower aircraft, such as the TBD "Devastators," to depart first in order to allow them to arrive at approximately the same time as the faster planes. The USS *Yorktown* air group at the battle of the Coral Sea used this method in 1942.

If haste was not a vital consideration, the CAG usually opted for a "deferred departure," meaning that the aircraft orbited the ship until all the aircraft had joined up properly and all squadrons of the air group were in their assigned positions.

Along the way to the target the pilots tested their guns and radios. Any operational failures, of weapons, radios, or engines, would force a pilot to return to his ship and miss the strike. Otherwise, flying to the target was generally a routine and tedious part of the mission. Approach to the target was usually made at multiple altitudes, with the bombers and their fighter escorts taking high station and the torpedo bombers flying at lower altitudes. To avoid being detected by the Japanese, the strike planes maintained strict radio silence. Thus each pilot and crew member was left largely to his own thoughts until the target area was reached.

Air strikes against land targets were often started by a fighter sweep over the enemy airfield. This tactic was designed both to catch any enemy planes that were aloft in the landing pattern and to suppress any possible fighter interception that might interfere with the strike. Among naval fighter pilots these sweeps of enemy fields were much sought-after missions. Surprise was generally complete; the enemy rarely had time to man their anti-aircraft guns fully, and it was often possible for fighter pilots to pick up easy kills on any Japanese plane still in the landing pattern as the strike came in. Good air group commanders had to make sure that these prime missions were rotated among the different pilots of the fighter squadrons, otherwise his fighters might become "ace happy" and try to avoid less glamorous escort missions.

By its very nature, an air strike utilizes hit-and-run tactics and is over swiftly. Successful raids pinpointed enemy strong points and neutralized them with massive force, eliminating a potential threat to the US Fleet and allowing other naval operations to proceed less hampered by enemy action.

Invariably losses occurred to the strike force, and many naval aircraft would be damaged or shot down by enemy fire. Nobody in the air group wanted to risk the possibility of becoming a POW on a Japanese-held island, so many heavily damaged aircraft attempted a perilous return flight to the ship. While the planes approached the carriers, the landing procedures were started and preparations were made to save as many lives as possible.

The Landing Signals Officer (LSO), also known as "Paddles," was the officer responsible for landing the aircraft as quickly as possible. His hand signals communicated the corrections that the landing aircraft needed to make in order to land safely (December 1944). (National Archives)

The flight surgeons and corpsmen made all their preparations to receive incoming wounded. Lt. Cdr. Samuel Sherman explained the preparation that his ship, the USS *Franklin*, made for the reception of wounded airmen returning from a strike:

> I had a number of big metal containers, approximately the size of garbage cans, bolted down on the flight deck and the hangar deck. These were full of everything that I needed – splints, burn dressings, sterile dressings of all sorts, sterile surgical instruments, medications, plasma, and intravenous solutions other than plasma. The most important supplies were those used for the treatment of burns and fractures, lacerations, and bleeding. In those days the Navy had a special burn dressing which was very effective. It was gauze impregnated with Vaseline and some chemicals that were almost like local anesthetics. In addition to treating burns, I also had to deal with numerous casualties suffering from severe bleeding; I even performed some amputations.[13]

When the returning aircraft approached the carrier, they would take up positions around the ship in an orbiting pattern. Aircraft with seriously wounded crew members were given priority in the landing sequence. At the same time, the carrier turned into the wind and the signal "prep Charlie," indicating that landing operations were about to begin, was flown at the dip of the signal yardarm. The Landing Signal Officer (LSO) took his position at the stern of the ship, and control of the landing procedures was passed to him. Each landing aircraft made a series of left-hand turns as it orbited the ship prior to making its final approach. The pilot normally saw the LSO, dressed in his characteristic yellow shirt, as he ended his third turn, and entered the "groove"(the final approach to the ship). The LSO directed the pilot by means of a set of signals and body gestures amplified by his signal paddles. With gear, flaps, and tail hook all down, the aircraft received the signal for "cut"; the pilot cut his engine RPMs and the tail hook caught the arresting cable. Plane movers in blue shirts pushed the plane to the forward end of the flight deck. The strike was over.

With the formal surrender of Imperial Japan aboard the USS *Missouri* in 1945 the US Navy had grown into the largest fleet the world had ever seen. The 65,000 naval aviators trained between 1940 and 1945 had battled adversity and weathered the initial losses of the war to make a significant contribution to the final victory of the Allied forces over the Axis. In the coming years the Navy, with carrier battle groups, would become the first line of defense for America.

"Lord guard and guide the men that fly." For many aviators and crew, death in combat was a grim reality of war. Here men of the USS *Intrepid* CV-11 are buried at sea following their death in a kamikaze attack (November 1944). (National Archives)

MUSEUMS AND COLLECTIONS OF INTEREST

San Diego Aerospace Museum
2001 Pan American Plaza, Balboa Park
San Diego, CA. 92101
(619) 234-8291
www.aerospacemuseum.org

This is a must for the naval aviation enthusiast. The museum has a research library that is open to general researchers on appointment. The entire collection of 70 aircraft spans the entire history of flight with a special emphasis on the history of aviation in San Diego. Naval aviation is well represented with a display based on a carrier-deck setting with overhead and deck-level aircraft on display. Included are the following aircraft: N2S-3 Stearman "Yellow Peril," F4F-4 Grumman "Wildcat," F6F-3 Grumman "Hellcat," SBD-4 Douglass "Dauntless," PBY-5A Consolidated "Catalina," and A6M-7 Mitsubishi "Zero."

Planes of Fame
7000 Merril Ave.
Chino Ca. 91710
(909) 597-3722
www.planesoffame.org

This collection of 150 aircraft contains many unique and hard-to-find examples. Of particular note is the museum's collection of Japanese aircraft, many of which are one of a kind. On the first Saturday of each month the museum features a special seminar that showcases one of the Planes of Fame collections. Included in the seminar is a flying demonstration of the aircraft. Naval aircraft in the collection include: A6M-5 Mitsubishi "Zero" (Flying condition), A6M-5 Mitsubishi "Zero" (static display), J2M Mitsubishi Raiden "Jack" (static display), J8M1 Mitsubishi Shusui (rocket fighter), G4M-1 Mitsubishi "Betty" (crash site display), D3A2 Aichi type 99 "Val," SBD-5 Douglas "Dauntless" (flying condition), F4U-1 Vought "Corsair" (flying condition), FM-2 General Motors "Wildcat" (flying condition), TBM General Motors "Avenger" (flying condition), F6F-3 Grumman "Hellcat" (flying condition), and F6F-5 Grumman "Hellcat" (flying condition).

National Museum of Naval Aviation
Naval Air station Pensacola, Florida
www.naval-air.org

This is the US Navy's official location that houses their collection of aircraft and memorabilia. The scope of the collection is from the birth of US naval aviation to the present day, and contains over 140 aircraft.

The museum houses a variety of innovative exhibits, including a full-scale replica of the island of the USS *Cabot*, complete with aircraft ready to launch. The hangar deck exhibit takes the visitor into the work and crew spaces of an American World War II carrier with a look at the life of the crew.

One exhibit of note is the "Sunken treasures" display of two naval aircraft recovered from the bottom of Lake Michigan. The aircraft, an SBD-5 and an F4F-3, appear as they did on the bed of the lake.

The actual plane collection is far too numerous to list in full, but some previously unmentioned aircraft from this collection include: PB2Y-5R Consolidated "Coronado," PB4Y-2 Consolidated "Privateer," SB2C Curtiss "Helldiver," and F4F-3 Grumman "Wildcat" (non-folding wings).

The Private Collection
of John Peacher
Chula Vista, California
Peachair@tns.net

Following the return from a mission the non-damaged aircraft flew "racetrack" courses around the carrier until all the planes that had wounded men aboard were landed. (National Archives)

This private museum is dedicated to the uniforms and gear of the naval aviator from 1914 to 1950. Mr Peacher's collection has just about one of every item either worn or carried by the naval aviator. The collection focuses primarily on the flight helmets of World War II, with one-of-a-kind types as well as the helmets familiar to all war film buffs. The collection is open to viewing on appointment with Mr Peacher.

NOTES

1 Markey, Morris, *Well Done!* p 42.
2 *Ibid.*, p 46
3 *Ibid.*, p 52.
4 *Ibid.*, p 65.
5 *Ibid.*, p 51.
6 Bell, Sheridan, *Chaplain Bell interview*, file box 2, World War II interviews, Operational Archives Branch, US Navy Historical Center.
7 Sherman, Samuel, R., "Flight Surgeon on the Spot: Aboard the USS Franklin, 19 March 1945," *Navy Medicine*, 84, no. 4, July–August 1993.
8 Markey, *Well Done!*, p 63.
9 *Current Tactical Orders and Doctrine US Fleet Aircraft*, Vol. 1, Sec. 2203.
10 Tillman, Barrett, SBD *Dauntless Units of World War 2*, p 32.
11 Tillman, Barrett, *TBF/TBM Avenger units of World War 2*, p 37.
12 Markey, *Well Done!*, p 6.
13 Sherman, Samuel R., "Flight Surgeon on the Spot: Aboard the USS Franklin, 19 March 1945," *Navy Medicine* 84, No. 4, July–August 1993.

BIBLIOGRAPHY

Buel, Harold, *Dauntless Helldivers*, New York: Dell Publishing, 1992

Cline, Rick, *Escort Carrier WW II*, Placentia Ca: R.A. Cline, 1998

Hammel, Eric, *Aces Against Japan v.1, v.2*, Pacifica Ca: Pacifica Press, 1992

Harper, John A., *Paddles*, Atglen Pa: Schiffer Military History, 1996

Kernan, Alvin, *Crossing the Line*, Annapolis Ma: Naval Institute Press, 1997

Lundstrom, John B., *The First Team*, Annapolis Ma: Naval Institute Press, 1984

Lundstrom, John B., *The First Team and the Guadalcanal Campaign*, Annapolis Ma: Naval Institute Press, 1994

Markey, Morris, *Well Done!*, New York: Appleton Century Inc., 1945

Sherman, Samuel, R., "Flight Surgeon on the Spot: Aboard the USS Franklin, 19 March 1945," *Navy Medicine* 84, No. 4, July–August 1993

Tillman, Barrett, *SBD Dauntless Units of World War 2*, Oxford, Great Britain: Osprey Publishing, 1998

Tillman, Barrett, *TBF/TBM Avenger Units of World War 2*, Oxford, Great Britain: Osprey Publishing, 1999

Wildenberg, Thomas, *Destined for Glory*, Annapolis Ma: Naval Institute Press, 1998

Wooldridge, E.T., *Carrier Warfare in the Pacific*, Washington DC: Smithsonian Institute Press, 1993

In case of a bad landing the carrier had barriers installed to prevent the landing aircraft traveling too far up the flight deck. In the foreground is a firefighter, a "Hot Poppa," in asbestos fire suit. (National Archives)

GLOSSARY

ACTG Advanced Carrier-Training Group. A temporary assignment given to new pilots in order to give them further instructions in carrier landings.

AR Air rockets, weapons with 3–3.5in. warheads.

ASW Antisubmarine warfare.

AvCad Aviation Cadets, a rank applied to aviators prior to obtaining their wings and commissions as officers.

Black Box The link instrument trainer.

Black Hole of Calcutta The junior officers' berth aboard a carrier.

BuNav Bureau of Navigation, a branch of the Navy responsible for the training of naval aviators.

CAA Civil Aviation Authority. The precursor to the Federal Aviation Authority (FAA). A civilian government authority responsible for the licensing of pilots.

CAP Combat Air Patrol. Short-range mission flown by fighters to defend the Fleet.

Checks A term that refers to a flying skills test given to cadets during training.

CinCUS Commander-in-chief of the United States Fleet, later changed to Chief of Naval Operations due to the unfortunate pronunciation of "Sink Us."

Crossing Day A celebration where the ship crosses the Equator and naval personnel are initiated into the society of shellbacks.

Dumbo Air-sea rescue missions usually flown by flying boats.

FDO Fighter Direction Officer. The officer charged with the tactical deployment of fighters on CAP.

Gun decking Writing an exaggerated report.

IAP Inner Air Patrol. Long-duration search mission flown by escort bombers to search for possible submarine contact.

IFF Identify Friend or Foe. A radar beacon that allows ship radar operators to distinguish between friendly and enemy aircraft.

JATO Jet-Assisted Take Off. A small rocket pack that attaches to the hull of flying boats, allowing them to take off with heavy loads quickly.

LSO Landing Signals Officer. The officer that stands at the stern of the ship and directs the landing operations with signal paddles.

NAP Naval Air Pilot. The title given to enlisted naval personnel who have gained pilot status in the Navy.

NRAB Naval Reserve Airbases, also known as elimination or "E bases," where the naval aviator took preflight and primary flight instruction.

Pollywog A new sailor who has never been over the Equator before.

Shellback An old salt who has previously crossed the Equator.

TBS Talk Between Ships. A short-range radio to allow various vessels to communicate during maneuvers.

V-5 A training program of voluntary pilots conducted at college campuses across the USA.

Wardroom The room aboard ship where officers take meals.

COLOUR PLATE COMMENTARY

A: THE US NAVAL AVIATOR – UNIFORM AND EQUIPMENT

This illustrates the "classic" look of the naval aviator from the early through to the late stages of the carrier war in the Pacific. He wears the AN-S-31 khaki flying suit (Army-Navy standard), the M450-1 flying helmet, tan leather gloves, and russet leather aviator boots. During the course of the war many variations on this basic uniform were seen with each aviator having his own individual interpretation of regulation dress. The flying helmets were often embellished with distinguishing devices such as stripes, shamrocks, or even in one case a "yo-yo" complete with the item hanging from the back of the helmet. A close look at the right leg of the flyer shows a couple of personal changes that have been made to the uniform by the addition of a survival knife and sheath sewn directly onto the flight suit. These changes were not regulation, yet were common while on active duty. The collective term for these changes to personal gear was "rigger made," from the name of the ship's parachute riggers who often made them in return for money.

Helmet detail
1 M450-1 flying helmet.
2 Flight goggles and aviator sun glasses.
3 RS-76 throat microphone.

Personal side arm
4 The Smith and Wesson M&P (Military and Police) 38 caliber revolver. Pilots on some of the earliest air strikes against the

Plane crews had to move quickly to re-spot aircraft forward on the flight deck following a landing (1943). (National Archives)

Japanese went to extraordinary lengths, like wrapping their revolvers in waxed masking tape to keep them waterproof.
5 The russet leather shoulder holster with cloth ammo loops sewn onto the cross strap.

Early and mid-war pattern life vest, known as the "Mae West" after the buxom Hollywood star. Both patterns had self-inflating CO_2 cartridges as well as air tubes for emergencies.
6 Earliest pattern prewar self-inflating life vest, worn until 1942.
7 Wrap-around life vest, issued in the late 1930s, saw service throughout the war.

Standard parachute
8 The standard parachute for pilots of single-engine aircraft.

A spectacular 1943 picture taken aboard the USS *Enterprise* shows the devotion of the deck crews, as Lieutenant Walter L. Chewing climbs onto the wing of this burning VF-2 F6F to save Ensign Byron Johnson. (National Archives)

The parachute acted as a seat cushion while in the plane and attached to the back harness by means of large metal snap clips.

9   The standard aviation parachute harness and hooks. Note the white strapping common to most US Navy chutes.

B: LIEUTENANT THATCH'S 'BEAM DEFENSE' TACTIC

Ominous news of a new Japanese fighter appearing in China began to circulate amongst US Navy fighter pilots in the summer of 1941. Rumors of the new-type "Zero" said that it was both faster and more maneuverable then the current US fighters, the F4F Wildcat and the F2A Buffalo. If this were indeed the case, naval aviation would have a difficult problem to overcome. One US Navy officer took these warnings seriously; he was Lieutenant James Thatch, the commander of fighter squadron VF-3. Thatch knew that the Japanese Zero fighters out-performed his F4F Wildcats in several key areas, yet, formidable as these advantages were, he was confident they could be overcome. On the plus side was the rugged construction of the F4F and its powerful armament, and a powerful battery of four .50 caliber Browning machine guns mounted in the wings. In the words of Thatch himself: "I believed that we had good guns and could shoot and hit even if we had only a fleeting second or two to take aim. We had to do something to entice the opponent into giving us that one all-important opportunity; it was the only chance we had." (*Carrier War In The Pacific*, p10.)

Beginning at night and in his spare time, Thatch tried many different ideas. Sitting at his kitchen table in his home in Coronado, California, near NAS North Island, he got out his favorite tools, matchsticks, and used them to arrange what he termed his "beam defense" tactic. Simply put, his fighters were to operate in divisions of four planes further subdivided into two plane sections flying abreast of each other. The distance between the sections was to be the aircraft's turning radius. The remainder of the plan was remarkably simple: whenever enemy fighters attacked either section, both sections would break sharply toward each other. As the paths of the sections crossed, the enemy would have the choice either to break off

the attack on the beleaguered section or be shot at by the other section from a head-on position.

In order to test out his new tactic, Lieutenant Thatch had his division of Wildcats configured so that they would only be able to operate at three-quarter power. The attacking force, led by ENS Butch O'Hare, would operate at full power to play the part of the attacking force: "We went up and he made all sorts of attacks, and I think it looked like a pretty good thing to me. Every time he came up to attack we kept weaving away." (*Carrier War in The Pacific*, p 11.)

It was not until after the battle of Midway that the Thatch Weave became known to other members of the Fleet; eventually the Navy adopted the tactic officially as a part of its fighter training in *Current Tactical Orders and Doctrine, Carrier Aircraft* (1944 revision).

1   American section of two aircraft flying CAP with the leader in position slightly ahead and above his wing man.

2   A Japanese "V" of three type "O" fighters attacks the Americans from astern.

One important piece of equipment for dealing with damaged aircraft on a flight deck of the carrier was this motorized crane, known as "Annie" to the crew. The crane replaced smaller tractors that had hitherto been used for aircraft removal. (National Archives)

3   Rather than becoming involved in a "dogfight" with the Japanese the American section begins "The Weave" a maneuver where the American fighters make sharp 45-degree turns towards each other.

4   As the Americans turn the Japanese follow, making a standard zero deflection shot from astern of the lead American fighter.

5   The chase continues but now as the Second American fight completes "The Weave" he may fire on the Japanese trailing the lead American plane.

6   The Japanese fighter is now faced with the dilemma – take the punishment from the .50 caliber machine guns of the American fighter or dive away to safety.

C: ATTACK OF THE VB-6 ON *HIRYU* – BATTLE OF MIDWAY

Pictured here is the attack of VB-6 on the Japanese aircraft carrier *Hiryu* at the battle of Midway. Following the successful

Low fuel or battle damage often forced pilots to ditch near the carrier as this VF-47 pilot found out the hard way. (National Archives)

Admiral Halsey allowed aviators and aircrews "medicinal" brandy following harrowing missions. It was in the keeping of the ship's flight surgeons (June 1944, USS *Monterey* CVL-26). (National Archives)

morning attacks by the aircraft of TF16 and 17 on the Japanese Fleet a second strike was ordered to attack the one remaining Japanese aircraft carrier. A mixed bag of 24 SBDs from *Yorktown* and *Enterprise* attacked the *Hiryu* at 1700 hours. *Hiryu* was struck by four 1,000 lb bombs on her forward flight deck, the last of which being delivered by Lieutenant Richard H. Best of VB-6, USS *Enterprise*, the subject of this plate.

The SBDs pictured in the plate are painted sea gray on the upper surfaces and light gray on the underside. The national insignia on the wings and fuselage have had the early-war red circle and alternating red and white rudder stripes removed. This order went into effect in the middle of May 1942 before the battle of Midway, due to the number of friendly fire incidents earlier in the war.

D: LANDING OF AN F6F

The Landing Signals Officer (LSO), also known as "Paddles," conducts the landing of an F6F in this plate representative of a mid-1943 scene. Landing operations especially under battle circumstances were some of the most dangerous aboard the entire carrier. The LSO stands on an exposed platform on the port side stern of the carrier. By visual signals delivered by means of his highly visible paddles the LSO was able to communicate a wide variety of landing instructions to the pilot; some of these signals were mandatory, the "wave off" and the "cut" telling the pilot to cut his engine so that it would not endanger deck crew rushing to move the plane.

Standing behind the LSO is the Flight Deck Officer (FDO), often known as "FLY 1." This officer, usually a senior lieutenant or lieutenant commander, was the man in charge of overall direction of the deck of the carrier during flight operations. All members of the FDO staff including the LSO and the plane handlers wear the distinctive yellow deck jerseys, so that they can be picked out at a moment's notice. In this scene the FDO checks the performance of the new LSO in his duties of landing aircraft.

Located in the gun gallery is a member of the arrester cable team (so designated by his green deck helmet and jersey). This individual's job was to assist in the disengagement of the aircraft tail hook and help to reset the hydraulic arrester cable

prior to the next landing. Landing operations could get quite hectic when the interval between landing was short.

E: PREPARING AIRCRAFT FOR LAUNCH

The organized chaos of preparing aircraft for launch aboard an Essex-class carrier in August of 1943 is the topic of this plate. Looking astern from the "island" superstructure, the Commander Air Group (CAG) looks on as a chief petty officer (CPO) supervises the various members of the deck crew in spotting aircraft on the flight deck. These Curtiss SB2C Helldivers are man-handled into place prior to take-off. In the near foreground a yellow-shirted plane handler gives the pilot of the plane a hold prior to passing him off to the next handler further up the deck.

The second of the SB2Cs in the plate shows one advantage that the Helldiver had over the Dauntless, namely the folding wing design. In spite of the SB2C's folding wings the plane was far from easy to handle, earning it the nickname "Son of a Bitch 2nd class" among the plane pushers.

The deck crew of the carrier was a group of highly skilled teams that were responsible for the arming, launch, moving, spotting, catapulting, and recovery of all the planes in the air group. These individuals were distinguished by their own special-color helmets and deck jerseys: yellow for the plane handlers, blue for the plane movers, green for the catapult and arrester crew, and red for the ordnance gang.

F: DEALING WITH A CRASH LANDING

The nightmare of all pilots and members of the deck crew was a crash landing of an aircraft. Stocked with aviation fuel and bombs, the aircraft carrier was high vulnerable to fire. Indeed three of the four Japanese aircraft carriers at the battle of Midway were lost when they were hit with bombs during flight operations, resulting in their destruction.

In this summer 1944 scene aboard an Essex-class carrier, deck crew rush to rescue the pilot of a Hellcat as an ordnance

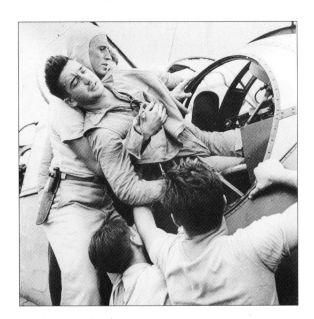

For many wounded men the trip home was agony. Here plane handlers remove an aircrew man from his TBM. (National Archives)

crew member (in his red jersey) races to carry an armload of 3.5 in. rockets away from the flames. A white-suited fire fighter, know as a "Hot Poppa," gets a curtain of water between the flames and the cockpit of the plane. Other members of the deck crew would make sure that the aviation fuel lines were flooded with CO_2 in order to prevent a massive explosion.

G: EMERGENCY LANDINGS

Many aviators were not fortunate enough to reach the relative safety of the carrier's flight deck and were forced to land somewhere at sea. USN emergency equipment had steadily improved as the war progressed, and more lessons were learned in the art of survival. All American aircraft were provided with a life raft, emergency rations, flare gun, signal mirror, and weapons. Yet often these pieces of equipment were lost in the course of the evacuation of the stricken aircraft.

The allied commanders of the Pacific battles went to great lengths in planning rescue operations to recover pilots that had been forced down at sea. Prior to any air operation, map coordinates were planned where rescue submarines would be located; in this way pilots might try to reach a safe haven in case they had to ditch.

If everything went wrong and the pilot had to bail out close to a Japanese-held target, then the last resort was the PBY Catalina flying a "Dumbo" mission. Named after the popular cartoon character, these "Dumbo" flights would land their flying boats close to the aviator, pull him in, and then take-off, often under enemy fire.

H: US NAVAL AVIATOR OF THE SOUTHERN PACIFIC ISLAND CAMPAIGNS – UNIFORM, EQUIPMENT AND INSIGNIA

The American musical *South Pacific* conjures up images of tropical island paradises, warm waters, and friendly natives.

The reality of war in the southern Pacific was a good deal different, with mosquitoes, malaria, and dysentery being more the order of the day. The central figure of this plate is an American aviator of these island campaigns dressed in the standard Navy khaki working uniform with russet flying boots. The pilot has made some concessions to the heat by rolling up his shirtsleeves and turning his work trousers into shorts. At the feet of the aviator sits the USN issue officer's valise, the most common piece of personal luggage carried by naval aviators during the war.

This aviator's gear is of a fairly standard pattern for late World War II, consisting of an OD web pistol belt, a Mills cartridge pouch for a .45 caliber Colt model 1911, and a russet leather holster and automatic pistol. One additional piece of equipment that has been added is a USMC-pattern machete and scabbard, a very necessary item of equipment on a tropical island with its dense vegetation.

Personal and survival items

1 The Mae West, a new standard model for both the Army and the Navy.

2 The flashlight, standard Navy issue, made of brass.

3 The "survival" vest is an USAAC-pattern Emergency Sustenance type C-1. A unit construction with built-in pouches for rations, cartridges, personal items, gloves and a pistol holster.

Weapons

4 M1928 M1A1 Thompson sub-machine gun and 30-round box magazines.

5 M 1 carbine with 15-round magazines.

6 Colt M1911 .45 caliber pistol.

Rank insignia and badges of the naval aviator

7 Wings of the naval aviator.

8 Wings of the naval flight observer.

9 USN cap device.

10 ID tags.

11 Rank insignia of the Navy:

    a Admiral; **b** Vice Admiral; **c** Rear Admiral; **d** Captain; **e** Commander; **f** Lieutenant Commander; **g** Lieutenant; **h** Lieutenant Junior Grade; **i** Ensign

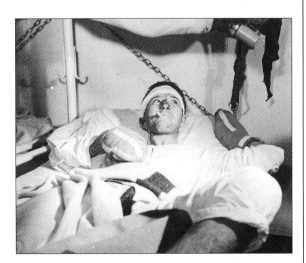

The most common injuries aboard ship were burns. Here a wounded sailor has been evacuated to one of the Navy's floating hospitals for return to a rear area. (National Archives)

INDEX